BAR

KEYS TO YOUR CHILD'S HEALTHY SEXUALITY

Chrystal de Freitas, M.D., F.A.A.P.

BARRON'S

Cover photo © TSM/Roy Morsch

All inquiries should be addressed to:
Barron's Educational Series, Inc.
250 Wireless Boulevard
Hauppauge, New York 11788
http://www.barronseduc.com

Library of Congress Catalog Card No.: 97-50485

International Standard Book No. 0-7641-0298-2

Library of Congress Cataloging-in-Publication Data
De Freitas, Chrystal.
    Keys to your child's healthy sexuality / Chrystal de Freitas.
        p.   cm. — (Barron's parenting keys)
    Includes bibliographical references (p.   ) and index.
    ISBN 0-7641-0298-2
    1. Children and sex—United States.   2. Sex instruction for
children—United States.   3. Sex instruction for youth—
United States.   I. Title.   II. Series.
HQ784.S45D4   1998
649'.65—dc21   97-50485
                                                                              CIP

PRINTED IN THE UNITED STATES OF AMERICA
987654321

CONTENTS

Introduction

When should I start talking to my daughter about menstruation? How much information should I provide my preschooler about the conception, growth, and birth of a new sibling? Why does my son think he knows so much about the "birds and the bees" when he is only eight years old? The family-rated television show was loaded with sexual innuendoes. Should I have insisted that we turn it off? How carefully should I monitor my children's entertainment in the future?

These are just a few of the common concerns that we parents face as our children interact with a culture that bombards them with sexual messages. Understanding the broader dimensions of sexuality and the roles that family, friends, school, and the media play in influencing children's views of themselves as sexual beings is essential for charting a safe, smooth course through the potential minefields between childhood and adult sexual identity. Many parents wait to address sexual issues until their child enters puberty. Obvious bodily changes in their youngster force some parents to deliver "the talk." Others hope the school will do what they don't want to and are relieved when their child returns home clutching pamphlets handed out during a lecture on sex education. Moreover, most parents have not had much education in the field of human sexuality themselves. They may have vague memories of awkward speeches by one or the other of their parents; the book about human sexuality tucked in the back of the bookcase; or the week devoted to reproduction in health class. Given this set of circumstances, it is understandable that parents often put off educating their own offspring. Many parents also believe that if they don't talk about sex, their children won't be interested or tempted. But waiting until puberty to approach the topic of sexuality is unwise. Sexuality is an important part of children's lives from the moment they are born and plays an important role throughout their entire lives. Providing children with the information that allows them to make informed choices and be the architects of their own lives is the essence of parenting.

Talking about sexuality requires the same communication skills that contribute to all healthy relationships between parents and children. If parents can cultivate open dialogues with their young children as they explore the topics of sexuality together, this same openness will allow parents to offer advice and guidance as their youngsters approach teenage years. However, if parents do not begin the process early, the subject of sexuality will feel less natural for both parents and their children, and everyone involved may be uncomfortable with this new intimacy and with the sheer magnitude of the issues that must be dealt with in a hurry. But keep in mind that starting late is far better than never starting at all.

As a pediatrician and mother of three children, I, too, have struggled with communicating "how-to's," with the various versions of the birds-and-the-bees talk, and with the many dimensions of sexuality. The challenge has been difficult. Prior to my oldest daughter's taking a girls' health class at school, I casually inquired about the health curriculum. Her answer disturbed me. The curriculum seemed insufficient to me, and was to be taught by the male gym teacher. Even though he was a nice person, I felt uneasy for my daughter, and I sheepishly volunteered my services. My offer to teach the class was readily accepted, but I felt sudden anxiety as the relieved teacher showered me with gratitude and handed me the scant curriculum. I faced many hurdles while preparing to teach such an important class. Perhaps my greatest challenge was broadening my own perspective of sexuality. The topic is much more comprehensive than it appears at first glance. Sexuality includes not only the nuts and bolts of human reproduction, but encompasses relationships, values, and many life skills as well.

As I taught the health class, I was struck by the students' reluctance to use their family members as resources. Comments such as, "I am too embarrassed to speak to my mom about this," were common; yet these young girls were willing to ask a stranger for answers. There was a chasm between mothers and daughters, between parents and their children. I sensed a need to unite family members in the educative process. This urge led to my establishing a community class for mothers and their daughters during which we reviewed the normal physical and emotional changes of puberty. I discovered that mothers delighted in the opportunity to review the basic physiology of their daughters' bodily changes and were eager to share their concerns with other mothers about the emotional turmoil they experienced with their maturing daughters. Similarly, girls in the class had an opportunity to participate with their mothers, forming a bond, a bridge of communication, during an interactive, educational process. For some families, this class was a start. Although it is best not to wait until puberty, there is certainly a window of opportunity during these prepubertal years to open the door of communication about sexuality and to share your values with your children. Imagine classes where fathers and sons could share similarly; or, why not a class where both parents attend with their children?

During the course of the past three years, I have asked parents to share their thoughts and feelings with me about the topic of sexuality, as they see their daughters and sons enter puberty. Most of them had heartfelt thoughts to express as they completed the following sentence: "The one message I would like my preteen to know about sexuality and/or growing up is. . . ." Some of their responses follow.

- "In spite of the discomforts, embarrassments, confusion, conflicting feelings, and mood swings that accompany puberty, it is truly wonderful to grow into womanhood. I hope that being female, expressing yourself as a sexual being, and having the potential to bear children will make you as happy as it has made me."
- "Sexuality is essentially who you are. It's your whole person and it continually develops over a lifetime."
- "The act of sexual intercourse and/or sexual intimacy is best shared by two loving adults in a mature and committed relationship, and, when experienced this way, it's a wonderful and cherished time."
- "Dad and I love you so much, that you can always come to us. You are the most important person in our lives and we will always answer your questions."
- "If you choose to become a husband and father, I hope that you will enjoy those occupations as much as I have and will remember that you and your wife are a parenting team made up of two loving people who should always work in the best interest of close family relationships."

My hope is that the information in this book will provide parents with a blueprint that will help them address the topic of sexuality with their children at the different levels of development, from preschool age through the preteen years. Presenting information in incremental steps through open communication and dialogue should help parents and their children build informed, trusting, healthy relationships. By proactively addressing common issues confronting children and their sexuality, you and your children will have built the foundation necessary for their development into healthy, sexually responsible adults. This accomplishment is the reward for choosing to take active roles in our children's sexual education.

This book could not have been written without the input of the many parents and youngsters who have attended my parenting and puberty classes. It is because of them that my motivation flourishes. I would also like to thank my friends and colleagues Eileen Bond, A.C.S.W., Karen Christian, M. D., Jill Michel, Sioban D. Harlow, Ph.D., and Allen Dumont, M.D., and his wonderful staff for their continued support and enthusiasm for this project. In addition, I offer my gratitude to the editors at Barron's, Grace Freedson and Linda Turner, for their aid and advice during this project, and to my illustrator, Jane Schlesinger, for her artistic talent. Most of all, I am indebted to Kathy Roby, whose skilled editorial pen has been invaluable. Last, but not least, thanks to my children, Cecily, Jocelyn, and Andrew, (who, I hope, know that they can always come to me with their concerns, even though they still roll their eyes whenever they hear me mention sex and insist I don't talk to them about sex in front of their friends), and to my husband, Jeff Bonadio, M.D., for his encouragement and sense of humor.

The information presented in this book is based partly on the *Guidelines for Comprehensive Sexuality Education* prepared by the National Guidelines Task Force of leading educators, health professionals, and national organization representatives. These *Guidelines* were made available through SIECUS (Sexuality Information and Education Council of the US). Their "Key Concepts" outline has been invaluable in organizing this material.

1

▲▲

UNDERSTANDING SEXUALITY

For many parents, teaching young children about the birds and the bees is the first step toward fulfilling their responsibility to provide sexual education for their offspring. Many parents, though, lack a clear understanding of the complexities of the word *sexuality*, often mistaking it for the word *sex*. Sexuality comprises more than physical sex or gender identification; sexuality plays a vital role in the development of every human being. Understanding sexuality includes understanding how the human body functions and, in particular, how reproduction occurs. Sexuality also includes an array of concepts related to human relationships, personal life skills, gender identity, and choices about health issues. In addition to teaching their children what they want them to understand about sexuality, parents must constantly run interference between their offspring and the influences of society and the media, which often threaten healthy family values. Clearly, learning about sexuality is a complicated and lifelong process.

Children are born with a natural curiosity about all aspects of their environment, including their bodies. This heightened awareness of bodily functions starts during the early toddler years and continues throughout puberty. Children who know how their bodies function will have a better understanding of their sexuality and a stronger sense of identity. Knowledge empowers children. Therefore, children, as well as young adults, must have reliable information available to them, either through the family or through other resources in the community.

Along with biological knowledge, children need to learn about personal relationships. They rely upon their families and the dynamics among family members as they put together all the pieces of their sexuality. Since friends, teachers, and other acquaintances become vital parts of any child's world, learning the life skills to cultivate and maintain successful relationships is essential. Children who are members of close family alliances gain powerful tools through examples provided by each family member. These tools help them to forge future relationships outside the family. It is within the family that these early skills are practiced with parents and siblings. Therefore, parents should be aware of the powerful influence familial patterns of behavior have in establishing their children's future relationships.

A healthy sexuality goes hand in hand with a set of values and morals that give direction and purpose to life. Children need opportunities to learn and practice life skills based upon moral principles learned and practiced at home. Making responsible decisions, communicating feelings and needs, and negotiating conflict are skills essential to successful adult life. They provide children with the foundation for maintaining and enhancing self-esteem; and they help ensure youngsters' healthy lives. Cultivating sound moral values can help children make better choices as they grow into young adults and are confronted with demanding issues such as deciding the when and how of sexual activity, grappling with teen violence, and avoiding date rape.

In addition to behavioral influences, children learn about gender roles from their families and from society. Gender roles are the whole realm of behaviors that are associated with maleness or femaleness. The gender roles that society writes for individuals can be very powerful and can influence choices about relationships and health that will determine a child's future. Children have a keen ability to detect parental and societal attitudes about values and beliefs concerning sexuality. The more comfortable parents are with themselves, including their own gender identity, the more comfortably they will project their own sexuality.

In addition to behavioral, moral, and gender-role identities, children must learn about sexually related health concerns. Today, more than ever, parents, educators, and health care providers are painfully aware of the need to provide accurate information to young adults about HIV/AIDS and STDs (sexually transmitted diseases). Often information from one source conflicts with that from another, or is woefully outdated. Children hear about these topics on the playground, through the media, and (perhaps, if they are fortunate) in school health education classes. Growing children will have increasingly detailed questions about HIV/AIDS and STDs, and parents, as well as school personnel, should review pertinent facts with them regularly. In addition, parents must actively learn and convey new, relevant information about these diseases to their kids.

Another influence upon the sexuality of the child is the media. TV, magazines, and video games constantly portray attitudes that become incorporated into a child's frame of reference. These messages may not always be consistent with your family's values. Parents need to take active stands at home and publicly on the quality and content of the media that can and will influence their children. In general, the media overemphasizes sex, presenting very confusing, conflicting, and diverse messages to children. The influence of the media on our children's lives has reached overwhelming proportions.

With a better understanding of the complexities of sexuality, parents can help their children grow up with solid self-esteem and a core of knowledge that will allow them to become sexually responsible adults.

Keys to a healthy sexuality:

- All human beings are born with the capacity to experience sexual feelings.
- Children are sexual beings from the moment they are born.
- A healthy sexuality is a vital part of a child's healthy self-esteem.
- Your example as a parent provides a model for the development of your child's sexuality.
- Providing children with information appropriate to their developmental stage is essential to their sexual understanding of the world.
- Sexuality affects the physical aspects of our bodies as well as the emotional aspects, including relationships, life skills, and decision-making skills.
- Children receive information about sexuality from the media, their peers, and society in general. We parents do not necessarily agree with all of this information, but we need to prepare children to cope with it.
- Parents need to provide their children with clear messages regarding their own family values and attitudes about sexuality.

2

SECRECY VERSUS PRIVACY

When talking to children about sexuality, secrecy and privacy take on new meanings. Young children may not be able to comprehend the subtle distinctions between these two terms. Therefore, parents should be very explicit when attempting to differentiate between *privacy* and *secrecy*.

Private body parts is a phrase that children can learn and use when talking about their genitals. Many preschoolers will repeat these words very comfortably without feeling the embarrassment that older children do. So an important issue for parents is how to keep the level of embarrassment low enough, as their children grow older, that neither they nor their children are unwilling to seek information when they need it. I believe the key lies in understanding the difference between privacy and secrecy and by realizing the empowerment that comes with knowledge. Kristy Seibold, the health education teacher for the public school district in Lansing, Michigan, presents a laudable instruction to help children relax as she speaks to them about sexuality. It can be summarized as: "Don't be embarrassed by knowledge!"

Let's take the word *secret*. Most children giggle at the use of this word and have a clear idea of the meaning of a secret, and what it means to keep a secret. A secret is something that only a few people know, and it should not be shared with anyone else. Obviously, if one shares a secret with others, it is no longer a secret. It loses its value if everyone knows about it. So a secret is something that not everyone is allowed to know, and one is not supposed to tell.

Private information, on the other hand, is information that *is* allowed to be known, but not necessarily shared. For instance, all families have *private* matters. We know that about each other's families, and they know it about ours. The main distinction, then, between *private* and *secret* is that private means limited access. Even though all families have private matters, we do not share them with other families. We make choices to keep things private for good reasons. The access to these matters is limited to family members. Similarly, everyone has private body parts, but we have access only to our own and not someone else's. We cannot touch someone else's private parts unless we are given permission.

To clarify these distinctions for your children, you could use the following example: A person's home and all the possessions inside it are private. Everyone knows that you have a home, TV, furniture, and so forth, but very few people are allowed access to your things. Your home and your stuff are private. Others have TVs, too. But you cannot walk into someone else's house and watch the news on their set. It is theirs. It is private property. Do not touch! Another example is a party. Most parties are private parties. Many people may know there is a party in progress, but not everyone is invited to it, because it is a private party. Attending requires an invitation.

For young children, talking about privacy with regard to using the bathroom may be easier to understand. Everyone knows that we all have to use the bathroom. This information is not a secret, but it definitely is private. How does it have limited access? We close the door when we are in the bathroom. In addition, no one laughs or makes fun of someone who is going to the bathroom because it is something everyone does. It is not a secret that we go. But we know going to the bathroom is a solitary activity. It is private. We use a door to limit others' access when we are in the bathroom, just as we limit others' access to the private parts of our bodies by wearing clothing.

Many children and preteens giggle and are embarrassed when they talk about issues of sexuality. Perhaps their discomfort is because they feel sexuality is a secret issue. But we parents can clarify that everyone is a sexual being, even members of the opposite sex, and so knowing about sexuality is never something to be embarrassed about. Knowledge helps everyone understand each other better, and may help take away some of the embarrassment. Never be embarrassed by having knowledge!

Sexuality is a private topic, and we each decide who in our lives we will share it with. So, for the preschool and the preteen youngster, parents should say that, although they have shared knowledge about private topics within the family, this is not information that children should share with younger friends. Their friends' parents may want to be the first ones to talk to their children about private body parts, sex, and the birds and bees. Children need to understand that other parents may not share their family's values, and they may not want their own child to hear information from an "outsider." To teach your child what you want to be shared with others and what behavior is acceptable, role play the "what if . . ." game. "What if Jamie came to you and asked to see your private body parts, what would you say?" Or, "What if Brian asks what being gay means?" As a parent, you can offer your child a couple of simple sentences to have ready just in case a friend or "outsider" requests access to private matters. For example:

- My body is private.
- You should ask your parents about that.
- That is a great question, but the answer is very complicated.

A final thought about privacy versus secrecy has to do with learning. Parents are children's most important teachers. We understand that learning about sexuality is vastly important to our youngster's future health and happiness. But often, as we set about sharing information about the personal, private matters that will help them now and in the future, we feel nervous and embarrassed. We giggle. Our kids giggle. We shuffle and look over their shoulders. They do the same. Finally, we see the humor in this situation, and we laugh together. We are O.K. Giggling, embarrassment, and humor are just the accompaniments to the melody that sings its private truths about sexuality. Just as we all experience private necessities, we all experience our own sexuality in our own unique way. Everyone is sexual; everyone learns about sexuality. Therefore, if we parents whisper our messages to ourselves as we prepare for one of the "big talks," or feel embarrassed and giggle as we open the topic of sexuality with our children, we are just behaving normally—just easing the tension. It is the situation that causes our jitters, not the knowledge we will convey. We and our children must never be embarrassed about knowledge. We all have a right to know.

3

TALKING ABOUT SEX

T alking to children about sexuality feels overwhelming for most parents. Parents worry about saying too much or too little, or they are concerned about confusing their children. Many parents also feel that by telling their children about sex, they will plant sexual ideas in young minds and encourage experimentation. Still other parents assume that their children are too young or are not interested in this subject because they have not asked questions or shown any particular interest. Parents assume that this apparent lack of interest means the child is not ready, or, worse yet, does not need any information. But children *do* have questions. They may not know exactly what to ask; or, perhaps they sense their parents' hesitance to address questions. Both instances may cause the child to turn away from parents when dealing with the topic of sexuality. Therefore, it is your responsibility as parents to speak up. Do not let your own uneasiness or your child's silence get in the way of introducing the subject. Admit to your child that talking about sex may be embarrassing because it is such a sensitive and private topic; that may give both of you a common ground upon which to start a conversation. Keep in mind that you do not have to provide all the information at once. Just as other subjects, such as math or science, are learned in incremental steps, so is sexual education. Start out with the basic concepts, and then add to that foundation as your child gets older and is able to assimilate more detailed information.

Whether or not you have started talking to your children formally about sexuality, be assured that the informal process of their sexual education began the moment they were born. Since then, as parents, you have been nurturing their sexuality through the ways you treat them, the ways you meet their needs, and by your own examples. It is important to realize that your children have been learning about sexuality all along without your direct help. Furthermore, their sexual education will continue whether or not you have decided to be an active participant in it.

Every time your children watch TV, play with toys, or interact with peers, they receive messages about who they are, their roles and feelings as girls and boys, and about society's expectations of them. All the elements in children's environments play roles in establishing their sexuality. All contribute to their perceptions of themselves. Unfortunately, many of the unspoken messages that our society conveys to children may not be based on values and beliefs that promote healthy adult sexuality. So do not hesitate to plunge in and add your own contribution. It is never too late to start. After all, everyone else is influencing your children; why shouldn't you? You have an obligation to convey your feelings and values. As a parent, you are still your child's most important teacher.

Teaching children about sexuality may seem a monumental responsibility, but there are many resources in our present society that can help you with your child's sexual education. Some are valuable; others are questionable. Family members can prove invaluable in reinforcing information presented by parents, and sources like schools, churches, and organizations (such as Girl and Boy Scouts) can contribute by providing bits and pieces of information to your child. (See Additional Resources). Finding an appropriate balance by which children learn the necessary facts and values from respected adults, while filtering the mixed messages of our society, is a challenge. It is imperative not to forget that sexuality is an integral and beautiful part of adult life.

Finding Teachable Moments

Teachable moments are opportunities that occur during our daily lives and serve as openers for further conversation about the topic of sexuality. Car trips, when children and their parents are captive together but do not have to face each other, are good times to initiate conversations about sexuality. You can make any of the following a teachable situation.

- A teacher, family member, or neighbor who is pregnant
- A TV program depicting family values or divergent family morals
- A trip to the zoo that includes observations of sexual behavior between animals or instruction about their life cycles
- A family pet who has given birth
- An upcoming visit to the doctor's office for a routine check up
- Teens holding hands or kissing in public
- Your child staring at naked or partially clothed bodies at home, at the swimming pool, etc.
- Your son or daughter trying to catch a glimpse of another person in the nude
- The curious stares of your child while you are changing an infant's diaper
- Seeing sanitary pads or tampons at the grocery store

My Child Has No Interest in the Subject

If your child is five or six years old and has not shown any interest in the subject of sexuality, parents may need to take the initiative and approach the topics of sex and babies. There are several ways of doing this. Before you start, though, you should gather some information and figure out appropriate responses to possible questions.

- You may want to initiate the conversation about sexuality by simply relating a personal comment from your own life: "When I was growing up, Grandma never (or sometimes) talked to me about where babies came from. I'm wondering if you ever think about that?"
- You might be more comfortable using a picture book. Although eight- or nine-year-olds may feel that they are past the stage of picture books, a book can be a valuable tool for breaking the ice and may serve as a platform for further conversation. (See Suggested Readings.) I encourage you to read the book you select first, and then read it together with your child. Some children may prefer to browse through the book alone. This approach is less threatening to them and should be respected. At a later date, ask whether your child has any questions or comments about the book. This may open up some discussion. Of course, many kids will say, "No!" That's fine, too. Respect your youngster's sense of privacy, but your reassurance that you will welcome any questions in the future is very important. Without being preachy, let your child know your values and feelings about whatever issue you are reviewing.
- You might also use one of the teachable moments listed earlier.

Key Points to Remember When Talking about Sexuality
- A parent is a child's primary educator about sexuality.
- A certain amount of embarrassment is normal when you begin talking about sexuality with your child.
- Your children need a reliable source of information and the ability to communicate with you or a trusted adult about this very sensitive topic.
- If you feel uneasy, speak with other parents and practice your comments and responses aloud.

- There are innumerable teachable moments in the day that you may seize and explore with your child.
- Age-appropriate books or literature about sexuality that conform to your family's values should be available to your children.
- It is acceptable to postpone the answers to questions if you are caught off guard; but don't forget to get back to your child with the answer soon.
- Information about sexuality, just like any other topic, needs repeating. One talk is not sufficient.
- If you feel you made a mistake during a talk with your child, tell the child you were wrong and fix the error. You may want to start out with: "Remember when we were talking about babies? I did not give you all the right information. I did some reading about it, and this is how it really goes."
- Humor goes a long way in easing tension and bridging the communication gaps between parent and child.
- Ask older, middle-school children if they have any comments about their health class.
- Get involved in the health education program in your community and its schools.

4

THE NEED TO KNOW

At each age, there is basic information about human sexuality that a child should know and comprehend. Therefore, a review of guidelines for age-appropriate information should be useful.

By age five, most children should have some basic concepts about the following topics. They should

- know the correct names for their body parts, including genitals. (See the review of terms in Key 8.)
- understand the simple basics about where babies come from, that is, from the mother's womb or uterus. (See Key 5.)
- be aware of the concept of personal privacy while dressing or using the bathroom. In particular, five-year-olds should understand the difference between secret and private.
- be comfortable talking with parents or a trusted adult about the subject of sex.
- have good self-esteem concerning their female or male identity.

As children get older, more information should be added to their basic foundation of knowledge. Usually, though, before you offer new information and ideas, a review of previous concepts is a good strategy. No matter how clear you believe you have been, your child may have forgotten or missed something important.

Between the ages of six and nine, most children are able to comprehend the following concepts. They should

14

- understand the reproduction of animals and plants as a part of the life cycle.
- have heard about the "facts of life." Where do babies come from? How do babies get in? How do babies get out? (See Keys 5, 6, and 7.)
- be aware of the differences between the sexes. Be able to use the correct terms for their genitals and those of the opposite sex.
- understand concepts related to families: parenting, divorce, and remarriage.
- have some basic understanding about HIV/AIDS and other sexually transmitted infections. (See Keys 33 and 35.)
- be progressively more responsible for the basic health and safety needs of their bodies, that is, personal hygiene such as brushing teeth and taking showers, practicing appropriate eating habits, and so forth.
- have a sense of what constitutes friendship and fairness, and be able to communicate their feelings to parents or trusted adults.

If you have not started talking to your child about sexuality by age nine or ten, it is not too late, but it is important to do it soon. Children are always in a better position to handle change if they are prepared beforehand for what will happen in the future. Unfortunately, many parents wait until their child begins to experience the physical changes of puberty before they introduce the topic of sexuality. Although better late than never, the earlier you start, the less likely embarrassment will sabotage your conversations. Parents who have visited the topic of sexuality often, even if briefly, have a better opportunity to teach their preteens and to remain involved during a crucial time in their sexual development.

During the ages of nine to thirteen years, most preteens can comprehend and should be familiar with the following:

- Sexuality as a normal part of life
- The normal changes that both boys and girls will experience during puberty (e.g., girls menstruate and boys may have wet dreams.)
- How to make and keep friendships (usually of the same sex)
- The reproductive process, including the meaning of terms such as *sexual intercourse, parenthood, abortion, contraception*
- The different sexual orientations: straight, gay, lesbian, bisexual
- Additional information about the transmission of HIV and STDs
- A continuing sense of body privacy and knowledge about sexual abuse, including how to identify it, how to protect oneself from it, and how to react in potentially dangerous situations

Key Points

- At different ages, there is developmentally appropriate information that should be addressed.
- Children need to know that their parents or another trusted adult will be available to them to answer their questions without making fun of them, embarrassing them, or betraying their privacy.
- Children need answers to their questions according to their developmental age. The younger the child, the more matter of fact or concrete your answer needs to be. Two or three brief sentences, at the very most, are all they may need. Preteens require more information, which can be found through books, brochures, or formal classes.
- As a parent, you can help your child by having a clear sense of your own personal values about sexuality.
- Children need to see that the important adults in their lives behave responsibly in relationships within and outside the family.

16

5

WHERE DO BABIES COME FROM?

S ooner or later, your child will ask the question, "Where do babies come from?" You may be caught unaware, and the question explodes like a bombshell in the grocery store, when in-laws are visiting, or at the pool as your innocent youngster stares at your pregnant friend. Depending on family dynamics, a parent may escape this query with: "Go ask your mother"; "You're too young to understand that"; or "I'll explain it to you when you get older." The unspoken message is that the subject of procreation is off-limits, taboo. Parents' fears about addressing a child's curiosity probably stems from the fact that they hear the youngster's questions from an adult's complicated perspective (one that includes all the implications of sexual intercourse, love, sexually transmitted disease, unwanted pregnancy, the pain of childbirth, etc.). In addition, parents are concerned about whether their child is old enough to process the information offered without misinterpreting it or being overwhelmed by it. Parents routinely tend to overprotect their children, minimize their queries, and play down their interest. Children easily pick up on a parent's reluctance to talk and, what was once set aside to protect the child's innocence, is now viewed by the child as an attempt by the parent to avoid embarrassment.

Parents sometimes also feel reluctant to talk to their children about sex because of their own values or beliefs. What if, after they explain the facts of life, their children use the information for sexual experimentation? And what if children interpret their parents' willingness to talk about the facts of life as their condoning early and inappropriate experimentation? But parents' fears may be allayed by the results of credible scientific research. Providing children with a greater store of information has not proven to increase the degree of sexual experimentation among teenagers. In fact, kids who know how their bodies work and understand issues of sexuality are more likely to postpone sexual intercourse until a later age. Therefore, parents can set aside their fears and be assured that children benefit most when they receive sexual information from caring adults, that is, their parents. Children *will* satisfy their curiosity one way or another by seeking information through other sources such as friends, magazines, or television. They *will* also use their imaginations, which usually are more vivid than reality. We parents must direct our children's sexual education in order to ensure their healthy growth into adults.

One of the keys to successful sexual education is to remember that your child's learning is a gradual process. Not all the details should be presented at once. The accumulation of knowledge and facts should be continuous and must be repeated many times. A child's degree of understanding is much simpler and more concrete than an adult's. As the parent, you are the best judge of your child's level of development. The conciseness of your answers when addressing the first questions about the facts of life should depend upon your assessment of your child's ability to process the information you offer.

Review the following responses to children's questions about where babies come from and choose the ones you feel most comfortable with. Of course, you should feel free to add your own statements.

When a child under the age of five asks, "Where do babies come from?" the response should be kept simple and brief. A maximum of two or three sentences may be all that is needed to satisfy a preschooler's curiosity. But before you leap into the simple explanation, make sure that you know exactly what it is that your child is asking. Repeat or clarify the question for your youngster and for yourself. In other words, always start by rephrasing your child's concern. This also reassures you that what you think they are asking is what they really want to know. The following old joke illustrates this concept.

> Christopher, age four, races in, breathless, and asks his mom : "Mom, where did I come from?"
> Mom catches her breath, panic stricken, and worries, "Why now? I haven't reviewed the 'birds and the bees' yet. This is too much too soon!" She cleverly tries to buy time and inquires, "What do you mean when you ask, 'Where did you come from?'"
> Christopher looks up, puzzled, and says: "Peter said he came from Cincinnati, and I wasn't sure where I came from!"
> With a sigh of relief she responds, "Well, you came from Seattle."

Mom got a reprieve. This scenario is humorous, but the real one will come up sooner or later!

In Anne C. Bernstein's book, *Flight of the Stork,* children were interviewed about their ideas about where babies come from. Bernstein refers to some children between the ages of three and seven as "geographers." These children believe that babies have always existed. It is just a matter of going to the hospital, store, or elsewhere to pick them up. Knowing how children of certain ages think can help you address your child's questions more appropriately.

For example, parents need to clarify that babies are not bought at the hospital, but that the doctor, nurse, or midwife helps the baby come out of the mother's body. Many children are told that babies grow in the mother's tummy. It may seem logical to a child to equate food, tummy, and baby-growing. Nevertheless, this information is inaccurate, confusing, and difficult to correct later on. Children will cling to their underlying beliefs until their level of cognitive development allows them to absorb any new information that is given to them; therefore, new, accurate concepts may need repeating often, using different scenarios in order for them to be fully assimilated. This approach sets a solid foundation that allows the learning process to continue. It is no different from learning a new language. Repetition. Repetition. Repetition.

The following example illustrates a starting point for you and your child.

> Madeleine, age five, comes home after a full day at kindergarten.
> Madeleine: "Mom, where do babies come from?"
> Mother: "Where do you think babies come from?"
> Madeleine: "I'm not sure; maybe the hospital. But Mrs. Wilson is having one."
> Mother: "A baby grows in a special place inside a mother's body until it is ready to come out."
> Madeleine: "In your tummy, right?"
> Mother: "No, the special place is called the uterus or womb."

You may want to show your youngster that the uterus is just below a woman's belly button.

This explanation will satisfy most preschoolers. Nevertheless, some may want more information and may continue to quiz you further about the particulars of the *where* and *how*. Others are quite satisfied with less and lose interest. Many may repeat their own versions of your explanation during the next several days, perhaps choosing an inopportune occasion to do so. The joys of parenthood!

6

✳✳✳

HOW DO BABIES
GET OUT?

C hildren believe many fallacies about childbirth. For many young children, the most logical explanation of birth is that the baby somehow comes out through the mother's belly button. Even for the older child, the concept of birth is confusing.

When the topic of childbirth arises, it should be addressed calmly, with minimal descriptive detail. Simple clarity is important. The following brief explanation may help guide you. You may use some of it, all of it, or, perhaps you will develop your own version according to your child's level of understanding.

- The uterus, or womb, is like a balloon that can expand to make room for the baby to grow.
- When the baby is ready to come out, the mother's body helps her push it out. Babies are born through a special opening between a woman's legs called the *vagina.* Another name for vagina is *birth canal.*
- When the baby is ready to come out, Mom and Dad (or another support person) go to the hospital, and the doctor (or midwife) helps the baby come out of Mom's body.
- Sometimes, for many different reasons, a baby cannot come out through the vagina. Then it needs extra help.

21

- In this case, the doctor must make a cut on the mother's lower abdomen and bring the baby out through it. This is called a *Cesarean Section.*

Many children enjoy hearing stories about their own birth. Parents may use this ideal occasion to talk about the birth process. There is no need to understate the birthing experience. A healthy respect for the wonder of nature is essential. After all, the miracle of childbirth is truly awesome. A common early question among children is: "Does it hurt to have a baby?"

As a parent, you should answer truthfully: "Yes, it does! But mothers are so happy to see their new baby that they quickly forget about the pain; and there are ways of helping mothers to manage their discomfort."

Explanations about childbirth should be kept simple and concise, always leaving room for further clarification. Long, detailed explanations are unnecessary unless you are prompted to offer them by the nature of the questions your child asks.

Will I overwhelm my child if I explain the details?

Even if you do go overboard with a lengthier explanation than is warranted, your children will absorb as much as they can. The rest is simply lost. They will signal your excessive instructions by losing interest, appearing bored, or simply by moving on to another topic or activity. Most children's questions can be answered in three concise sentences.

Here are additional keys to keep in mind when talking with children about sex.

- Clarify what your child is asking. It also may be helpful to get a sense of the origin of his or her curiosity. Was it the TV, a pregnant teacher, or what a friend said on the school bus?

- Clearly state the facts that answer the question and clarify your beliefs. Two or three sentences for the very young child are sufficient. Add more information as your child gets older.
- Have your child repeat in his or her own words what you said.
- Be aware of your unspoken body language. A grimace, an overreaction, or an angry disposition will determine whether your child will view you as an "askable parent." Your attitude can set the stage for future communication about sexually-related issues.
- Admitting your embarrassment to your child (should you feel it) is humbling and often results in a bonding experience between parents and their child.

7

~~~~~~

HOW DO BABIES GET IN?

O lder children, ages five through eight, may not be satisfied just knowing where babies grow and how they get out. They also may be curious about how they got there in the first place. Their questioning may become more insistent as they try to elicit answers to this newest concern. Older children in this age group are aware of the need for both a male and female to make a baby, but they have many misconceptions about the father's role in the whole process.

Young children can certainly begin to understand that it takes a mommy and a daddy to make a baby. This concept can be simplified for them by reviewing the need for an egg cell from the mother and a sperm from the father to join in the mother's body in order for a baby to start growing. Another word for egg cell is *ovum,* a Latin word used when speaking about the eggs in the woman's ovaries. The singular term is *ovum,* the plural, *ova.* Parents may elect to use *egg cell* if they prefer it to ovum.

The current advice is that, although an explanation about fertilization using the word *seed* may seem simple, it leaves room for misunderstanding. Children at a young age are very concrete in their thinking. A seed to them is more or less like a pumpkin seed, just as "egg" means a chicken's egg that we purchase at the grocery store. In a child's world, a seed grows into a plant, and eggs are breakfast-fare. Therefore, to a child, these terms may have different meanings. Commonly, parents explain fertilization this way: an egg comes from the mother; the sperm from the father; when they meet inside the mother's body, a baby starts to grow. I gave this explanation to my own son. He laughed raucously as he declared the process "impossible." If the egg were inside Mom, certainly it would crack. Voila! No baby! Clearly, my information was completely wrong. Although children may not remember the grown-up words ovum and sperm, using them will certainly prepare children for the additional information they will receive later on. And using the biological terms may prevent confusing scenarios like the one I have just described.

Try asking your children where they think babies come from. You'll be surprised at the responses. This is an opportunity to clarify misconceptions. For instance:

> Child: "How do moms make babies?"
> Parent: "That is a wonderful question. Have you noticed that Aunt Wendy is having a baby?"

This question allows you to gather your composure, and it also sends the message that you are willing to talk about this sensitive subject. You might continue by asking, "Where do you think babies come from?" This question permits you to explore the child's ideas and helps clarify any misconceptions they may have. Then you can proceed as follows:

> "A woman's body has a special cell for making babies. It is called an ovum. It is as tiny as a pencil mark. Fathers also have special cells that are there only for making babies. A father's cells are called sperms. When these two types of cells join in a woman's body, a new baby starts to form."

Or you might answer the *how* question:

> Parent: "Well, it takes two people to have a baby. A man and a woman—a mother and a father. The father has sperm cells and one of those joins with one of the woman's egg cells. When these two kinds of cells join in the mother's body, a baby starts to grow. Now you tell me what I just said."

After the child repeats what you have said, she or he might ask:

> Child: "What is a cell?"
> Parent: "A cell is a very tiny, special, living part of our bodies. It is so small, you need a microscope to see it. When two tiny cells join, the ovum from the mother and the sperm from the father, a baby can start to grow inside the mother's body."
> Child: "But how do they get together? How do the sperms get inside the mom?"

This child has just asked a question that rattles many parents, because now they must explain the details of how the ovum meets the sperm. If it is clear to you that your child is asking about how babies are made and the mechanics of sexual intercourse, here is a simple version that can serve as a stepping stone:

> Parent: "A mother and father should decide they want to have a baby. They lie very close together, and they have loving feelings toward each other. The father's penis fits into the mother's vagina, and the sperms leave the father through his penis. A sperm joins the mother's ovum in the uterus. This is called sexual intercourse"

Many parents worry about the possibility of even more explicit questions, fired in succession. They ask themselves, "What if we appear as nervous as we feel? What if we do not know the answers?" Many youngsters' queries require answers related to morals and values about human sexuality. Parents must struggle to find the right words to convey these very important value-related messages to their children. Some comfort may be found in the ever-increasing body of literature about sexuality. Your wholehearted commitment to learn along with your child is worthwhile.

Although there is no one right way to discuss and define sex, here is a possible version that you may want to use or alter to suit your own personal style. Additional information can be added or deleted depending on your child's age, maturity level, and questions.

Various explanations of the word *sex* are as follows:

- There are many different meanings for the word sex.
- Sex can refer to whether you are a boy or a girl. It can also mean sexual intercourse.
- Sexual intercourse is an adult behavior.
- Sex is when a man puts his penis inside a woman's vagina.
- Sex is the way adults make babies.
- When two adult people love each other, there are many different ways of being sexual besides sexual intercourse. There is hugging, kissing, and intimate touching.
- Sex is a way in which two adult people who love and care about each other very much share their bodies in a very special manner.
- Sexual activity is when a man and a woman share their private body parts.
- Sexual intercourse feels good and is pleasurable for two adult people who care about each other sexually.
- It takes the maturity and responsibility of both adults to share their bodies in this very special way.
- Sexual intercourse is also known as *making love,* or *going all the way.*

As children get older, between the ages of eight and twelve, they acquire new levels of understanding and are able to comprehend that several ingredients must come together in order for a baby to be made: the concept of love and relationships, sexual intercourse, and a rudimentary interpretation of the sperm and ovum meeting. They are also able to understand that sexual intercourse involves a man and a woman sharing their bodies. This is the stage when parents need to establish their value systems and share them with their child. A window of opportunity exists during prepuberty when youngsters still listen to parents and value their opinions.

Key Points to Share with Children about Sexual Intercourse

- Sexual intercourse is the way a man and a woman reproduce—in other words, make babies. It's when a man puts his penis in a woman's vagina.
- Sexual intercourse may occur between two people who love each other and have a committed relationship with one another.
- Sexual intercourse involves big feelings, big actions, and big consequences. All of these intertwine with major responsibilities.
- Sexual intercourse can be a vital part of married life.

This is the time you should discuss specific values and religious beliefs related to sexual intercourse and sexuality in general.

8

━━━━━━━━━━━━━━━━━━━━━━━━━━━━━━━━━━━━

ANATOMY 101

"I clearly remember asking my mother about my genitals. I must have been three or four years old. She said, 'That's your girl.' I heard the word clitoris for the first time in college, Biology 101. It was quite a shock." (Forty-five-year-old mother)

Between the ages of one and five, when children grow very rapidly, they must absorb and assimilate a vast amount of information and understanding about the world around them and about themselves within it. They feel a natural curiosity about how the body works and what it is capable of. Gaining knowledge about their bodies empowers children and provides them with a sense of security. Toddlers are eager to please and ready to learn the names of their various body parts, including their genitals. Typical games that parents play with children, as they teach them to identify the components of their bodies, should include such terms as the *eye, nose, penis,* and *vulva.* Parents may be reluctant to use such adult words when speaking with their children about the private parts of their bodies, but why shouldn't youngsters learn the right words from the very beginning? It is twice as hard and just as embarrassing to relearn the correct names later on. Using euphemisms may give children the unspoken message that something is not quite right, that the genitals are unspeakably private or shameful and should not be mentioned openly. Since parents may not have played the identification game when they were children, they may experience discomfort as they pronounce and repeat anatomically correct terms to their offspring.

In spite of these worries, a simple lesson in anatomy *can be* lots of fun for most preschoolers. They usually giggle as you review the names of their various body parts. Go ahead and giggle along with them because this will help break the tension and keep the youngsters interested. Take this opportunity to create a teachable moment by reviewing the appropriateness of body privacy.

The following is a list of definitions of the parts of the genitals for your review. Most preschoolers can name those genital components noted in Figure 8.1.

Female anatomy

Genitals—a general name that refers to parts in your private area. This word applies to both girls and boys.

Vulva—the correct word describing the female genitalia that can be seen with the naked eye. Use vulva instead of "down there" or "vagina."

Mons—the portion of fatty tissue that covers the pubic bone.

Labia or lips—the folds of skin that cover the female genitals. Just as the lips on our faces keep germs out of our mouths, the labia protect the inner organs. There are two sets of lips, the outer (labia major) and the inner (labia minor) lips.

Clitoris—the small protrusion that you will see if you gently separate the labia. You may decide how to describe it to your daughter based upon your level of comfort. For example, "This is a very sensitive part of your body, and you will learn more about it as you get older." Or, "This is a very sensitive part of your body that usually gives you good feelings when you touch it."

**Figure 8.1
The female genitalia**

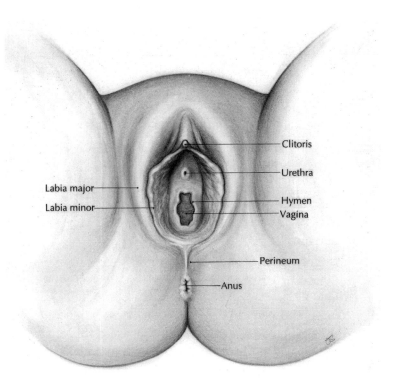

Urethra—an opening right below the clitoris through which urine comes. It is connected to the bladder, a balloon-like structure that holds urine in the body. It is somewhat difficult to see because it is so small.

Vagina—the next larger, easily visible opening. This is also the birth canal. (Children younger than five or six don't need to know the entire birth process at this time; that will come later.)

Hymen—a thin lining of skin around the edges of the opening to the vagina.

31

Perineum—the portion of skin between the vagina and the rectum. (You may want to review here the importance of wiping properly.)

Anus—the opening where bowel movements (B.M.) come out of your body. *Bowels* is another word for your gut or intestine. As food is digested, waste products, or feces, or "poop," are moved through the body until they come out the anus. Hence the term bowel movement, or B.M.

Buttocks—the two large muscles that cover the anus, also know as your "bottom."

Use this opportunity to review other parts of the body at the same time so that the genitals don't seem exclusive or taboo.

Male anatomy

Genitals—a general name that refers to the body parts in your private area. This word applies to both boys and girls.

Penis—the part of the body that hangs between men's legs. There are so many slang words for this organ that you may want to review with your child which ones he has heard. Help him select the one most comfortable for him, but keep in mind that, as he gets older, the word *penis* will be more acceptable.

Urethra—an opening at the center of the penis through which urine and semen leave the body, although never at the same time.

Glans—also known as the head of the penis. The crown or the part that is farthest away from where the penis attaches to the man's body.

Circumcision—a procedure, usually performed on an infant, during which a portion of the foreskin, also known as the *prepuce,* is removed. Take this opportunity to

Figure 8.2
The male genitalia

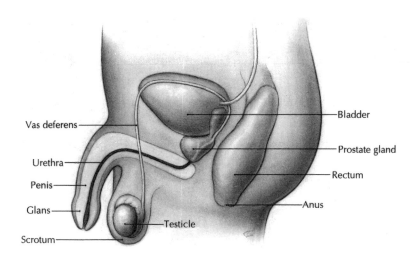

review with your son your religious beliefs or your family's preferences regarding circumcision.

Prepuce—the word for foreskin. This is the tissue that covers the penis. For boys who are uncircumcised, the foreskin should be gently retracted when washing to keep the penis clean. A natural secretion accumulates on the inside of the foreskin and should be cleansed away regularly. However, one should not attempt to pull back the foreskin roughly because this may cause pain.

Testicles—the two round or almond-shaped structures that hang below the penis. They are often referred to as "balls." Sometimes, one testicle may hang lower than the other, but both should be in the scrotum when relaxed.

Scrotum—the correct name for the sac-like tissue that holds the testicles.

Perineum—the space between the testicles and the anus.

Anus—the place where the bowel movements, feces, or "poop," come out.

Buttocks—the two large muscles that cover the anus, also known as your "bottom."

Vas deferens—the two tubes that allow sperm to pass from the testicles.

Rectum—the last part of the intestine, which connects to the anus.

Bladder—a sac-like structure in the lower abdomen that holds urine.

Prostate gland—a male gland located at the base of the bladder. It contributes a thin, milky fluid that makes up part of the semen.

Key Points for Discussing Body Parts with Preschoolers

- "Your body is a wonderful creation. It helps you think, have fun, and feel good."
- "Girls' and boys' bodies have lots of parts that are alike and some other parts that are different."
- "A boy has a penis, scrotum, and testicles."
- "A girl has a vulva, clitoris, vagina, uterus, and ovaries."

As your child gets older, or according to your child's developmental maturity, you may want to add other information. (See Key 30, Sexual Curiosity, for guidelines about nudity at home.)

9

BODY IMAGE

The earlier children learn to appreciate and value their bodies, the stronger will be the self-image they feel and project later as preteens, teenagers, and, finally, adults. Throughout early childhood, children constantly reach motor-skill milestones that should provide opportunities for reinforcing appreciation of their own bodies. Each time a youngster learns a new skill, such as riding a bicycle, playing soccer, swimming, or jumping rope, valuable golden moments arise for parents to point out how powerful, useful, and amazing the child's body is.

Children learn at a very early age that bodies differ in shape, size, and color. Not everyone is the same height. Some children are skinny, while others are heavy. Some children are Caucasian, some are African American, some are Hispanic, some are Asian, and others are a combination of races. All of these differences are parts of our heritage that should be celebrated. Parents are in a position to teach their children acceptance and pride in the diversity that our society has to offer.

A child's body is largely defined by heredity. Aspects such as body shape and skin, hair, and eye color are all determined by the appearances of the parents and grandparents. Physical characteristics can usually be tracked back to either the mother's or father's side of the family. In some families, children inherit a mixture of features from each side, such as their mother's nose and their dad's chin.

Most young children enjoy the fact that they resemble a particular member of their immediate family, especially if they share a good relationship with that person, and, particularly, if the two are the same gender. The feeling of belonging is a universal need that provides people with meaning and a sense of continuum.

Today's children are growing up in a society that idolizes thinness. Everyone is compared to a fantasy image of the "ideal" body. The media's representation of this perfect form is so far removed from reality that it borders on science fiction. Real people, the majority of society, in fact look very different from the "ideal." Yet the "perfect body" is portrayed everywhere: in magazines, in toys (such as Barbie and Ken), in TV ads for children, in books, and in videos. Parents and children are taught that there is no such thing as being too thin. It is an uphill battle for parents to disarm the message that thin is good, and we must step up to the front lines and teach that healthy is good. Children need to see that we parents accept our own body types and are not critical of others' bodies. Children should see that differences among people should not be teased or ridiculed.

Children between the ages of six to twelve learn to take on more responsibility for their everyday care as they grow. A gradual process of developing good health habits such as eating properly and exercising regularly adds to their sense of well-being. It also reinforces the concept that they own their bodies—bodies that ultimately are theirs to care for and feel good about.

As youngsters enter puberty, they all seem to have some dissatisfaction with their appearance. Some wish they were taller, or shorter; others want to have different hair—curly, straight, or wavy. Most are unsure of what they really want and anxiously wait to see how they will turn out. Many preteens are clearly ambivalent about the changes that occur during puberty. Some withdraw, becoming isolated, and struggle with the way they look and feel. Their bodies change in ways beyond their control, and if they do not settle finally into the perfect mold that is society's standard, they imagine the sky will fall. The bottom line is that most of the changes that take place *are* out of children's control. Physical appearance is predetermined by the genetic endowment of their parents. Of course, what kids eat can affect their appearance, but even obesity and acne are felt to have genetic components. However, healthy eating habits should be encouraged, mostly by parental example. Keep healthy food available at home, and practice moderation yourself. Your child will benefit as the machine that is his or her body runs smoothly.

Exercise can clearly influence the way the body looks, but will not change the body type. Nevertheless, it is especially important during the years preceding adulthood, that children learn and develop healthy lifestyles that can last a lifetime. Sports may provide an excellent outlet for making friends and developing a sense of belonging; and for those youngsters who are not athletic, there are other enjoyable and healthy activities such as walking, bike-riding, and jumping rope. Regular exercise promotes good physical and mental health.

Key Points
- Practice good eating habits at home.
- Encourage physical exercise on a regular basis. This can be through organized sports at school or local community centers, or by walking or bike-riding around the neighborhood alone or with friends.
- Praise and encourage everyday achievements related to physical growth. Simple acknowledgments about loss of baby teeth and the development of new, adult, permanent replacements are valuable.

37

- Share your family background with your child. You can do this by displaying family pictures, participating in family reunions, and so on. The sense of belonging to a greater circle of family is essential.
- Preteens are very interested in their physical appearance. Go shopping with them and help them select appropriate clothing. At times you may feel challenged. Keeping the peace in a department store dressing area can be daunting. Consider taking your child's friend along. Be patient and always end on a positive note such as sharing a treat.
- Take the time to point out to your youngster how unrealistic the advertisements in magazines, ads, and TV are. Most of these images have been retouched many times and do not represent the average human being.
- If your youngster seems particularly dissatisfied with his or her body, seek professional advice from your health care provider. Protruding ears, crooked teeth, and some birthmarks merit further evaluation.
- Praise all your children whenever you have the opportunity. When they are dressed up, take the time to point out how handsome or attractive each is. A simple compliment from parents can last forever in a child's mind.

10

WHAT IS NORMAL?

P uberty is that time when a child's body begins to change and develops the ability to reproduce. It is a natural, normal process that occurs in all human beings. At no other time, except during infancy, does the human body change so dramatically as it does during puberty. This is a period when parents begin noticing their child's physical growth, changes in body shape, and developing emotional independence.

Puberty can be nerve-racking for parents as well as for youngsters. Most parents are aware of the turmoil adolescence may bring, and many remember their own adolescent years with mixed feelings. Parents may bring into this phase of their children's lives their own perspectives of how it was when they were adolescents. For some parents, there may be unresolved issues, dating back to their own preteen years, that are stirred up as they see their child struggle with similar problems. A child's pubescence, then, may provide an opportunity for parents finally to deal with old business. It can be a time of growth, not only for the preteen, but also for the parent.

Parents who have enjoyed a really pleasant journey with their child through the youngster's early years may be saddened and chagrined as their newly adolescent child changes and begins an emotional separation from them. For others, the onset of puberty is a happy occasion because some parents find they enjoy relating to their child on a more adult level. Still, for others, concerns about potential risky behavior, possible decreasing school performance, and increasing societal pressures are heightened.

As boys and girls go through puberty, some of the changes they experience are similar, and some are different. The age at which puberty begins and ends varies greatly from one child to the next. Therefore, the ages that are offered here are all approximations. Each youngster will proceed at his or her own pace and should be reassured that that pace is just right.

For most girls, puberty begins around age nine or ten, although it may start anytime from age eight to fifteen years. If a young girl is fifteen years old and has not experienced any of the sexual changes associated with puberty, she should see a physician. The entire process of pubescent growth can take anywhere from one-and-a-half years to as long as eight or nine years to complete.

Most boys start their pubertal changes at age eleven or twelve. Here, too, there is wide variation. Male puberty can begin as early as age nine and as late as age fourteen. All the changes can occur over a short span of time, such as four years, or can take up to eight years to complete. The later the youngster starts to experience pubertal changes, the longer he will take to complete them. Some male adolescents continue to grow into their late teens. Both ends of the spectrum are normal. If a boy reaches the age of fifteen and shows no signs associated with puberty, he should be evaluated by a physician.

Though the timing of the changes that occur during puberty varies from child to child, the sequence of events is well known. However, the beginnings and the endings for the different transformations do overlap with one another.

Girls
A girl usually has some breast development and pubic hair before her first period, but adult breast size and mature

pubic hair distribution will not be completed until some time later. If a girl *does* have her first period before any breast development, she should be evaluated to make sure there is no underlying physical disorder. The sequence of events occurs in the following order:

- Breast buds
- Growth spurt
- Pubic hair
- First menstruation (menarche)
- Underarm hair
- Growth of uterus and vagina completed

Other changes, such as the development of acne and body odor, also may be noted and can occur at different times throughout puberty.

Boys

Boys start puberty shortly after girls do, usually at age eleven or twelve. Most of their pubertal changes overlap each other; therefore, several may occur at the same time. If a boy has excessive acne at age ten but has none of the other physical changes associated with puberty, he should be evaluated by his doctor. Boys' pubertal changes are more discrete than girls' and therefore not always as noticeable to their parents. The general order of development follows:

- Growth of scrotum and testes
- Growth of penis
- Growth spurt
- Pubic hair
- First ejaculation
- Voice change
- Underarm hair

Keys 11 through 19 review these changes in more detail.

11

~~~~~~

BREAST
DEVELOPMENT

The development of breasts is one of the earliest signs of puberty in about 85 percent of girls. Most girls develop breasts between the ages of nine and thirteen. There are well established guidelines for rating breast development called sexual maturity ratings. (These ratings also apply to pubic hair, which will be discussed later.) Breast development includes five stages, the first represented by the prepubertal girl with no breasts, and the fifth represented by the young woman with adult, fully formed breasts.

The progression through these stages of breast development is gradual. It can take four to five years to complete. Some girls, though, grow more quickly and reach maturity in one to two years. There is no way to speed up growth or, for that matter, to slow it down. Young girls may notice some small lumpiness underneath the nipple area in the very early stages of breast development. This area may feel tender, but it is, in fact, normal. Glandular tissue that will later contribute to the production of breast milk for nursing a baby is located there. It is also not unusual for one breast to grow larger than the other. This initial unevenness is common, and eventually both breasts usually grow to about the same size. Even so, it is not unusual for adult breasts to be slightly asymmetrical.

Some preteens worry about the size their breasts will be once fully developed. It is important to reassure your daughter that she will develop the breasts that are just the right size for her. Nothing that she does, or does not do, will influence the natural appearance of her breasts. Breast development is genetically predetermined, very similar to height, body shape, and eye color. Unfortunately, our society's emphasis on breast size as an attractive aspect of femininity is erroneous. Moreover, breast size has no impact on a female's ability to produce breast milk or her ability to have a satisfying sexual life.

As a general rule, once a young girl begins to notice her nipples protruding, or her breasts become tender, it is time to wear a piece of clothing between her chest and the outer layer. A camisole, training bra, or under-vest are available choices. Most girls are uncomfortable asking their mothers about how to deal with developing breasts, so mothers may have to take the initiative and suggest the next step.

A mother can turn this opportunity into a special occasion by going shopping with her daughter, getting her fitted for a bra, and then celebrating by doing something her daughter especially enjoys. Most large department stores have attendants who can suggest bra styles and help with measurements. It may take several trials before finding a bra that fits and feels comfortable, so don't be discouraged. Once breast buds are present, they will continue to grow over the next two years or more. Mothers can expect to go back to the store several times during this period to select new bras.

Many girls are very sensitive about the idea of wearing a bra, though there are those at the other end of the spectrum who cannot wait to wear one, whether or not they have any breast development at all. If she is sensitive about her growth, your daughter would be mortified if you told other people about her developing breasts and needing a bra, especially without her knowledge. So be considerate of her feelings. The following may be a conversational approach to try:

> "Hi sweetie, how are you? You know, I've noticed that you are growing so nicely these days. You are getting taller and your breasts are developing. Have you noticed?"

At this point, observe what your daughter's body language conveys to you. Is she embarrassed? Does she smile spontaneously; or does she fidget and seem anxious? Does she avoid eye contact with you? Has she perked up? Is she silently awaiting your next comment?

Continue your conversation by saying:

> "It may be a good idea to start wearing a bra. Have you thought about that?"

If she says, "NO!" do not insist. Put the subject to rest for a couple of weeks, and then bring it up again.

End by saying: "Will you let me know when you think you are ready?" Or, "Would you rather I ask you again in a couple of weeks?"

On the other hand, if your daughter responds enthusiastically, "Yeah, I want one. All the other girls in school are wearing them already," there is no better time than the present to go shopping together.

Most preteens are relieved to know that their mothers are paying attention to the changes in their bodies and are relieved, as well, that their mothers will probably notice if anything out of the ordinary occurs. However, not all kids feel positively about their parents' attentiveness to their development. If yours is one of the latter, be patient. No one ever said puberty is easy!

With breast development and additional underwear, comes an important opportunity to review with your daughter the fact that her body is private. Prior to puberty, most children have been told that no one should touch their private body parts, meaning those body parts covered by their bathing suits. For boys, this includes their genitals and their buttocks. For girls, it is their genitals, buttocks, and breasts. So when you talk to your daughter about breast changes and bras, make it a teachable moment to review the concept of privacy once again. During this discussion, assure your child that, at some time, when she is in an adult, loving relationship with another person, she will probably enjoy having her breasts touched. Emphasize that the choice is hers to make later on.

Teaching preteen girls about breast self-examination is generally not recommended. Breast cancer is extremely rare during the preteen and teen years. Given all the changes that accompany puberty, it is far too much to ask youngsters to take responsibility for self-examination to detect the presence of cancer. However, once young girls start their menses, or, no later than age fifteen, they should be taught about breast self-examination by a physician or a nurse, who will instruct them in the context of learning a good health habit rather than by scaring them about cancer. A teenager should be comfortable with her body and be able to note physical changes that may be significant. Performing breast self-examination should be presented as a way of taking care of her body, no different from using sanitary pads or brushing her teeth.

Boys and Breast Development

During puberty, boys also may experience some breast growth. It is not uncommon for a thirteen- or fourteen-year-old boy to notice lumpiness under his nipple area. These bumps can be pea-size, sometimes on one side or both. There also may be some breast enlargement known as *gynecomastia.* Both of these findings are entirely normal and resolve with time and reassurance. If the breast enlargement is pronounced or disturbing to the male preteen, parents should seek professional advice.

Commonly Asked Questions from Preadolescents and Appropriate Answers

"My breasts feel very, very sensitive. What causes this?"

"Your question is very important. First of all, it is very common for young girls to have sensitive breasts. This is normal. As you go through puberty, there are hormones that are responsible for the changes that occur in your body. These hormones tell your breasts to grow. As your breasts grow, the skin stretches, and you can feel pressure in them that makes them feel very sensitive. This discomfort will ease with time, but it may happen again during certain stages of your menstrual cycle, such as right before your period."

"Some people never wear bras. Ever! Do breasts really sag if you don't wear an undershirt or bra?"

"It's true that some people choose not to wear bras at all. This *is* a matter of choice. In some cultures, it's the custom to go bra-less. In our culture, it can be either way and may change according to fashion. With small breasts, not wearing a bra may be O.K. Most women with larger breasts wear bras for support and comfort, though. And bras may also keep your breasts from jiggling excessively when walking, running, or playing. Whether or not to wear a bra is a decision based on comfort. Plus, there's no evidence that wearing a bra will keep breasts from sagging later on. Because of gravity, most breasts do sag."

"Will I have small breasts like you do?"

"Since you and I look alike [or, you and your mother, if the father is answering], it's possible that your breasts will be a similar size. But there are many different sizes and shapes of breasts. Since you get your eye color, height, and all other characteristics from Dad and me [Mom and me], and we got ours from our parents, and they from theirs, you're a mixture of all of us. So, you may have breasts more like Grandma's than mine [Mom's]. We can't be sure yet. But we *do* know that however they turn out, they'll be just right for you."

Growth of her breasts is an integral part of a young girl's becoming an adult woman. Later, her breasts may provide nourishment for her newborn child. Surely, throughout their lives, our daughters will be bombarded by mixed messages from society about the importance of breast size and shape. We parents can nurture our daughters' healthy self-esteem by reminding them often that their breasts are just right for their bodies; they are private body parts; and they should be taken care of, as are the other parts of their bodies.

"Can exercise increase the size of my breasts?"

"Exercises builds muscle, but there is no muscle in breasts (they're mostly fat and glandular tissue), no amount of exercise can increase their size. But exercise such as swimming can strengthen the muscles that support your breasts. Remember, your breast size is determined by the genes that you've inherited from me and Dad [Mom and me]."

12

GROWTH SPURT

One of the unequivocal signs of puberty is a growth spurt. This growth is triggered by the emergence of sex and growth hormones in the body. As are most other bodily changes that occur during puberty, growth is out of our control. It is internally regulated by the genetic patterns that we inherit from parents. Most girls experience the beginning of their growth spurt around age nine, but a rapid spurt can start as late as thirteen. Boys' sudden growth can begin between ages twelve and fourteen.

Along with growth comes a new body shape. Curves around the hips become more pronounced as fat accumulates in response to hormonal changes in girls. The waist becomes more defined, and new body contours define a changing shape. In response to testosterone, a male hormone, boys develop more muscle mass, and their chests and shoulders broaden.

Appetites increase to enable new growth. Preteens require larger quantities of food to sustain the rapid transformation of their bodies. This is a time when children and their parents begin worrying about excessive weight gain. Battles over food can break out. By now, though, be aware that your preteen's food intake is strictly under his or her control. In fact, it has always been. Parents can serve as good role models by exhibiting healthy eating habits themselves; and they can stock the household pantry with nourishing choices. But how much children consume is up to them, as is what they eat when they are away from home.

Weight Gain—Girls

Before puberty, children gain approximately four-and-a-half pounds (2 kg) per year. But during puberty's growth spurt, 95 percent of girls gain between twelve and twenty-three pounds (5.5 and 10.5 kg) per year. The average is seventeen-and-a-half pounds (8 kg). Once a girl starts menstruating, her growth and weight velocity slow down, and she reaches her final adult height approximately two years later. Weight gain will fluctuate throughout life, but, to a certain degree, it is genetically controlled. Eating a balanced diet and keeping physically active are essential health habits that, if cultivated during this period of change, can last a lifetime. Girls' appetites may also fluctuate during their menstrual cycles. Increased appetites may be noted during the second half of their cycles.

Weight Gain—Boys

Boys do not exhibit a growth spurt until after their sex organs have begun to change. First, the testicles and scrotum get larger, followed by an increase in the width and length of the penis. Then, around age thirteen or fourteen, the growth spurt begins. This is about two years later than it is in girls. In addition, boys continue to grow for longer periods of time than girls do. This later, longer, growth spurt in boys in part accounts for the difference in adult heights, making most men taller than most women.

One of the changes during puberty that boys seem to enjoy most has to do with alterations in body shape. Their bodies tend to accumulate more muscle tissue on their shoulders, making them broader. Muscles also develop on thighs and arms, giving male youngsters more physical strength and agility. However, while boys are growing rapidly, their arms and legs appear lanky. It may seem to them and to their parents as though they have outgrown their bodies; they may appear clumsy and awkward as they adjust to their new body dimensions.

The weight gain for boys during puberty is approximately twenty pounds (9 kg) per year. Ninety-five percent of boys gain an average between thirteen and twenty-six pounds (6 and 12.5 kg). Just as for girls, there is an increase in appetite to accommodate this weight gain. During these years, healthy eating habits are of utmost importance to help ensure healthy patterns for adult life.

Shoe Size

Another impressive area of growth for both boys and girls is their feet. The feet may grow faster than other parts of the body and reach adult size before the rest. Some parents are concerned that their kids' feet will never stop growing. If a child wears an adult shoe size at age twelve or thirteen, boats may be required by the end of puberty. Luckily, feet grow more slowly during the later stages of puberty, reaching adult size before the rest of the body.

Voice Changes

Just as there is an increase in body size and weight, the voice box, or larynx, grows during puberty. This growth is responsible for the changes in voice register and tone and is noted mostly in boys. A preteen may hear his voice crack or sound squeaky, especially while singing. This change in voice tone is not something that can be predicted or controlled. In fact, in the beginning, the changing voice is most unpredictable. With time, the voice settles into an adult tone and range. For girls, the change in the size of the voice box is more subtle, and voice change is not as noticeable.

The *cricoid cartilage,* or Adam's apple, is a structure located in the midline of the throat. It is more pronounced in boys than in girls. During the growth spurt, the Adam's apple enlarges and becomes more prominent, especially in boys. But if your son's Adam's apple does not seem to grow, do not worry, because, although normal for some, not all boys experience this change.

Commonly Asked Questions from Preadolescents and Appropriate Answers

"Can you tell me how tall I'm going to be?"

"I was really anxious to know how tall I'd get, too. An old saying goes, 'Tall parents make tall kids, and short parents make short kids.' But this isn't always true. We *can* estimate how tall you'll be based on the way you've grown so far. We can use a growth chart to plot your height and weight based on your age. Then we can follow the growth curve to estimate how tall you'll become. We have one of these graphs in the front of your baby book. [We can ask the doctor to show us one of these graphs.] We'll plot your course. But remember, the chart isn't always right. We inherit our characteristics from several people, not just our parents.

Another way to estimate your final height is to add Mom's and my heights [Dad's and my heights] together and divide by two. Since you're a boy, we'll add two-and-a-half inches. If you were a girl, we'd subtract two-and-a-half inches. But remember this formula is not always right; but it is a good estimate. The best way to figure out your adult height is time. Just wait and see!"

"I'm short for my age, but I have already started my period. Will I ever grow taller?"

"Most of your rapid growth spurt happened before your first period. Remember how fast you grew? Now that you're menstruating, your growth has slowed down. You'll continue to grow a bit, though, and you'll probably reach your final adult height in about two years [two years from your first period]."

"How much does genetics have to do with my body shape, adult height, and weight?"

"Your adult height, breast size, and body shape are all predetermined by the genes you receive from Dad and me [Mom and me]. There's very little, if anything, that can be done to change the basic way bodies are shaped. Sometimes race, nutrition, exercise, and ethnic background can determine when you start your period and determine your shape."

Parents should consult their child's health care provider if they have concerns about their children's growth. But remember, not all youngsters develop at the same rate. Growth is regulated by hormones that, in turn, are controlled by genetics. Although weight gain and bodies that have not yet grown into their various parts are normal during puberty, kids are sensitive about these changes, and your reassurance is important to their self-esteem. We are role models for our youngsters, and our own healthy eating habits and projected comfort with our bodies will go far toward creating healthy, self-assured young adults.

13

BODY ODOR AND HAIR

Body Odor

As preteens move through puberty, all systems are in overdrive. Their bodies increase the production of perspiration and oil that secrete onto the skin's surface. Perspiration, or sweat, is a natural product the body produces as part of its cooling system. As the body's sweat comes in contact with the air, an odor results that is more noticeable, and perhaps offensive, to others than it is to the owner. Parents may notice their child's body odor as early as seven or eight years of age. Usually, preteens are not aware of their smell, and they may be insulted when it is pointed out to them. Nevertheless, a gentle reminder about the need to take regular showers and to use deodorants or antiperspirants is necessary.

Deodorants work by covering up the body's odor. Antiperspirants inhibit perspiration. There are many products on the market that combine both antiperspirant and deodorant properties. Selecting one is a matter of personal choice. Consider scent (or unscented), price, style (such as stick or roll-on), and endurance when choosing a product. Monitor your child for skin reactions when a deodorant or antiperspirant is first tried. If, after using the product for a day or two, your preteen develops redness and/or itching under the arms, he or she should stop using the product and wash the underarm area thoroughly. The irritation should improve after a couple of days. If it doesn't, consult with your healthcare provider. Luckily, allergic reactions occur very infrequently. Take time to tell your preteens when and how often to use a personal deodorizing product.

Oily Hair

There is also an increase in oil production on the scalp during puberty, which gives the hair an oily appearance. More frequent hair washing may be necessary—perhaps every day, or at least every other day; and you may need to remind your youngsters often that proper hygiene will require additional time and effort now that they are more mature. There are hundreds of products on the market, and most work well for keeping oily hair under control. Products that contain excessive amounts of moisturizer, though, may increase oiliness. Parents may want to guide their youngsters in choosing appropriate products that suit their specific needs.

Vaginal Odor and Discharge

In some girls, particularly those with extra weight, there may be some body odor noted in the genital area. This is normal and can be helped by a daily hygiene routine that includes a clean change of underwear. Cotton underwear tends to be more absorbent than other fabrics.

Several months before young girls start menstruation, they may notice a clear, stringy, odorless discharge from the vagina that may cause a yellowish discoloration on the crotch of the underpants. This is normal. It is the way the vagina cleanses itself. A vaginal discharge may also be noted during the menstrual cycle. Douches are not recommended for any age group since they may interfere with the body's own secretions and make the vagina susceptible to infection.

Body Hair

Shortly after the development of breasts in girls and after an increase in the size of the scrotum and penis in boys, hair will appear in new places on the body: legs, armpits or *axilla,* and in the pubic area. Hair growth is a gradual process and usually goes unnoticed by parents. Initially, pubic hairs appear as straight, dark strands. Eventually these strands of hair become coarser and curly. The final configuration of the adult female pubic hair is an inverted triangle. Pubic hair should not be shaved off. It will grow back, but, while it does, the underlying skin can become itchy and uncomfortable. Pubic hair may help to keep germs out of the genital area.

Pubic hair in boys first appears at the base of the penis and eventually covers the whole pubic area and up to the belly button in a diamond-shaped configuration. There is additional hair on the thighs, chest, arms, and face. For most boys, facial hair is a sign of manhood, and they look forward to shaving. Facial hair continues to increase at the sideburns, chin, and the rest of the face. Its growth is accompanied by new hair on the chest, back, and underarms. A boy's hairiness is another aspect of puberty that is predetermined by genetics.

Underarm hair—*axillary hair*—usually develops between the ages of twelve and thirteen in girls and fourteen to fifteen in boys. Hair growth in the armpits does not necessarily parallel the amount of hair that appears in the pubic area. In other words, a preteen may have quite a lot of pubic hair and very little axillary hair, or vice versa. Also the color of pubic hair may be different from the color of the hair on the head or under the arms. In some cultures, females do not shave their underarm hair, but, in others, it is more customary to do so. Whether or not to shave is a personal choice.

Girls and Leg Hair

Along with axillary and pubic hair, there is hair growth on young girls' legs. Most girls enjoy the commotion that arises around the decision: *To shave or not to shave . . . and when?* In the past, reluctant parents often allowed their daughters to shave only when they reached a certain age. This reticence may or may not be culturally based. Really, age is less important than whether or not the preteen is uncomfortable with hairy legs or is feeling pressured by her classmates or friends to shave. But regardless of how parents feel, girls at this age *do* need guidance early about the pros and cons of shaving, and it may be best for parents to bring up the issue instead of waiting for their daughters to broach the subject.

The following points should be clarified by parents when they speak with their daughters about shaving their legs.

- Once you start shaving, you will need to continue in order to maintain smooth legs. Although you may choose to let your leg hair grow out, it is a hassle. Stubs grow out slowly.
- Take care when shaving to use a clean razor and to avoid nicks and cuts, which can hurt and may become infected. Shaving requires your complete attention.
- Shaving cream or soap, spread on the legs before you shave them, may make the razor glide more easily and can give a smoother result. Also, as you shave off soap or creams, you can see where you've been and still need to go. Some shaving products cause skin irritation, so you may need to try several.
- Be sure your legs are wet when you shave them, or you will really irritate your skin.
- There are other ways to remove hair such as heated wax and electrolysis. Such methods are effective, but are more costly and must be performed by a trained person.

Finally, parents must decide whether or not the choice to shave now or later belongs to their preteen daughter. Parents might look at shaving as a positive step toward their daughter's independent care of her body. In any event, listening with patient ears to preteens' concerns about shaving will help ensure free-flowing dialogue when larger issues arise in the future.

14

~~~~~~

ACNE

A cne affects eight out of ten teenagers during the pubertal years, but can occur off and on throughout adulthood as well. Although acne may seem insignificant to the parent, it poses a real conflict for a young preteen who is already struggling with self-image and a changing body. So much is known now about the cause of acne and its treatment that there is no reason preteens or teens need to suffer physically or emotionally from it. Your children will benefit by your reassurance that acne is common and treatable. If you had it as a child, tell them you did and empathize with them.

Oil production, hormones, inflammation, and infection are the trademarks of acne. As preteens go through puberty, hormones are responsible for the increased production of an oily substance, called *sebum,* from oil glands that are located below the skin's surface. Sebum exits through skin pores to the surface of the skin. Often, skin cells stick together and clog the pores. Clogged pores and an excessive amount of sebum production set the stage for pimples and infection. When a pore gets clogged and the oil gland bursts underneath the skin, a pimple erupts. Sometimes the oily build-up under the skin becomes infected, causing pain and, in some cases, scarring. Before acne reaches this stage, seek professional help for your child from a physician or a dermatologist. The use of an oral antibiotic may be extremely useful in controlling serious cases of acne.

People get acne not only on the face but also on the shoulders, back, and chest. Sometimes oil-based shampoos and conditioners can cause acne along the hairline and on the forehead.

The best start toward a clear complexion is a clean face. Teach your preteens about washing their faces regularly with a mild soap, but be aware that acne is not due to dirt or oil on the skin's surface. It is the oil production *below* the skin's surface that causes pimples and acne. They should avoid using heavy-based oil products on their hair and faces as well. But if these measures are not enough to banish the skin's oily residue, or if pimples are already erupting, causing physical and/or emotional distress, it is time for a trip to the drugstore. There are several well-tested products that help prevent or, at the very least, minimize the presence of acne. Select a product that contains benzoyl peroxide. This ingredient has been shown to minimize the bacteria on the skin and lessen blackhead formation. It is present in a variety of gels, creams, and lotions. Concentrations of benzoyl peroxide can range from 2½ to 10 percent in over-the-counter products, but are available by prescription in higher concentrations. Another often-used anti-acne medication is *tretinoin,* a vitamin-A derivative. This sells under the brand name Retin-A, but is only obtained by prescription from a physician or a dermatologist.

These products all work by drying out the layer of oily skin, causing a mild irritation and sloughing of skin cells. Thus cells do not stick together and do not clog. The skin slowly flakes and peels, leaving cleaner skin in its place. Because these products may cause your youngster's skin to be more sensitive than usual, sunburn is a greater threat. Therefore, using a sunscreen is of utmost importance.

It is difficult to predict accurately which youngster is more apt to develop acne than another, but skin type certainly plays a role. Certain types of skin tend to produce more oil than others and, therefore, are more susceptible to acne. Furthermore, if parents struggled with acne during their teen years, the likelihood of their preteens having acne is high. On the positive side, though, oily skin tends to age better than dry skin. Oily skin wrinkles less.

Preteens and teens who develop acne and are contemplating using acne preparations need to be reassured that patience is extremely important. They may not notice improvement for four to six weeks and, sometimes, as long as three to five months. Above all, do not squeeze or try to pop the pimple. Popping them breaks the skin and can cause scarring.

Commonly Asked Questions by Parents about Acne

"What is a good face care routine for a ten-and-a-half year old?"

At this age, most youngsters only need to practice basic everyday hygiene. Washing their faces with mild soaps should be sufficient. This is a good time for them to learn to follow a healthy daily regimen. Learning to take personal responsibility for their own health habits before they become teenagers will reduce the amount of friction between kids and their nagging parents later on. Using astringents may dry up the excess oil on the skin surface, but will do nothing about the oil production underneath the skin. Facial scrubs irritate the skin and tend to increase the production of oil. Therefore, save your money and avoid using them.

"Does what you eat determine whether you'll have pimples or not?"

There are many of myths about acne. In the past, a popular theory was that chocolate or oily foods worsen acne. More recently, it has been demonstrated conclusively that diets do not influence the presence of acne. Oil glands, hormones, and bacteria are the culprits that produce pimples.

As dreadful as acne may seem to preteens and teenagers, parents can reassure them that today, more than ever before, there is help available that can minimize or totally prevent the emotional and physical scarring that otherwise will occur with untreated acne.

15

~~~~~~

MENSTRUATION

The onset of menstruation is an important event in the life of a young girl. It marks her passage into womanhood. Parents can make their daughters feel comfortable with this natural, monthly function by introducing the topic of menstruation early and often enough that their youngster's questions are completely addressed and any fears they have are allayed.

Before you attempt to explain menstruation to your children, they should have some basic understanding of the following concepts:

• The differences between male and female private body parts
• That a baby grows in the mother's uterus
• That it requires a male and a female to make a baby
• How babies get in and how they get out of a woman's body
• The meaning of sexual intercourse
• A clear sense of your family's values

If a child is eight or nine years old and theses topics have not been addressed, try to find a teachable moment in which to review the basics of reproduction. The concept of teachable moments is included in Key 3. You can start with a simple explanation about menstruation. For example:

• Menstruation, or having your period, is the way the female body practices for a possible pregnancy if and when she decides to have a baby.
• Menstruation happens to all girls when they start puberty.
• Menstruation is a very natural and normal part of growing up.

61

Based on the child's initial responses and their own levels of comfort, parents may want to add more information. If, as a parent, you are uncomfortable with the topic of menstruation, try reading about it beforehand. Review different approaches with friends who have youngsters of similar ages to yours. Many communities provide classes through local youth groups, hospitals, or churches that focus on puberty and menstruation. Attend a class with your daughter as a way of opening the doors of communication. Often schools offer a mother-daughter session with a visiting physician during the fifth grade. Parents can also provide their children with age-appropriate books on sexuality. (See Suggested Readings.) Follow these suggestions, and you are off to a good start. However, your parental responsibility has just begun. Children need to hear and review information about their sexuality many times throughout their preteen and teen years. Healthy sexuality is a lifelong learning process.

What and When

Menstruation is the hallmark of puberty for girls. *Menarche,* the first menstrual cycle, can occur anytime from age nine until as late as age sixteen. Menstruation is also referred to as "having your period." It is called a period because it occurs periodically, at specific time intervals. Most girls, when first told about their menstrual cycles, show some degree of disgust and/or preoccupation. It is important, therefore, for the parent to present information in a supportive and positive light, since menstruation is an intrinsic function of the female's body. A girl's first exposure to the topic of menstruation can leave a lasting impression on the way she views her own body in the future.

The onset of menstruation varies greatly from girl to girl. For the majority, menarche occurs once there is some breast development and after the appearance of pubic hair. A growth spurt will have preceded or accompanied these changes. No one can predict exactly when a girl's menstrual cycle will start.

Menstruation is regulated by a gland in the brain called the *pituitary gland*. The pituitary gland acts as an internal clock that awakens and signals the beginning of puberty at precisely the right time for each person. This gland sends messages in the form of hormones to the rest of the body. Hormones are substances within the body that are responsible for the changes associated with puberty, including growth and the development of reproductive/sex organs.

How and Why

The ovaries are the female's sex organs, and they produce one of the body's hormones, *estrogen*. Estrogen affects many organs and, at the same time, sends feedback to the brain until the appropriate balance among the circulating hormones in the body is reached. This very delicate and precise chemical balance is part of the wonder of the human body.

In addition to the production of estrogen, the ovaries serve as warehouses for another important female product, egg cells (ova). A woman is born with a fixed number of egg cells (400,000 to be exact!) that make up her lifetime quota. Triggered by the body's hormones, these ova begin to mature and are released from the ovaries. This process is called *ovulation*. Although several egg cells can mature at a time, usually only one ovum is released from the ovary during each menstrual cycle. At the same time, the uterus prepares for the possibility of pregnancy. (Remind your child that the uterus is the pear-shaped, balloon-like structure in the woman's body where babies grow.) The inner surface of the uterine wall forms a lining that will serve to nourish the potential fetus.

Once the ovum is released, it travels along the fallopian tube. If the ovum is not fertilized (which means an egg cell

Figure 15.1
The female reproductive organs

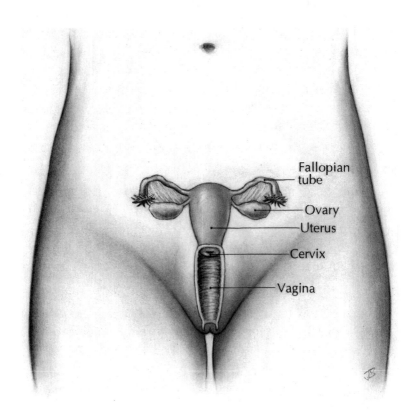

does not meet with a sperm cell), it travels toward the uterus during the next several days. Two weeks after ovulation, the dissolved ovum, along with the lining of the uterus, is shed. This lining, consisting of blood-tinged fluid, constitutes the menstrual flow.

The menstrual flow leaves the body through the *vagina*, the opening between the woman's legs that is also the birth canal. The menstrual flow can last from two or three days to as many as seven. The average is three to five days. There is approximately just one half-cup of blood lost, which the body replenishes naturally. The flow is a slow, steady trickle, as opposed to a sudden gush of fluid. The menstrual flow sometimes also contains blood clots and small pieces of tissue. The egg cell that was not fertilized is also expelled during menstruation, but because it is only the size of a pencil dot, it is not perceptible.

The menstrual cycle is recorded from the first day of the menstrual flow to the first day of the next one. Menstruation occurs approximately every twenty-eight to thirty-five days or, on the average, once a month. For the first year or two after menarche, though, many girls' menstrual cycles are irregular. This means some girls may skip several months in a row or have a period every two weeks, although the latter case is less common. Usually it takes an average of two to three years for the menstrual cycle to regulate itself to a more predictable schedule. Occasionally, it is not until after childbearing that menstruation becomes regular.

The Explanation

During their menstrual flow, girls use "feminine" or "sanitary" pads to absorb the liquid. These pads come in various styles, shapes, and materials and constitute the most popular product for young girls. Made of an absorbent material on one side and an adhesive reverse side, they fit nicely and securely in the crotch of underwear. Pads need to be changed about every four hours, depending upon the amount of the menstrual flow.

Another type of protection from menstrual flow is the tampon. These cylinders of absorbent cotton fit snugly into the female's vagina. The vaginal walls are made of muscles that are able to stretch and contract like a balloon when it is inflated or deflated. The advantage of tampons is that they make it possible for girls who swim and engage in other sports to feel confident about remaining active throughout their menstrual cycles.

Many mothers are concerned that the tampon may hurt younger girls or may damage their *hymens*. The hymen is a very thin layer of skin that partially covers the vaginal entrance. In the past, the hymen was associated with virginity. The truth is, for most young women active in sports, dance, or horseback riding, and even to the experienced eye of the gynecologist, it can be very difficult to detect the presence of a hymen. Although the tampon may stretch a vaginal opening a little, it is perfectly safe for young girls.

The different sizes of tampons are labeled according to their degree of absorbency: slender, regular, super, and super-plus absorbency. Parents can advise their daughters to start with the lowest absorbency needed to control their menstrual flow. If they soil their underwear after an hour or two with that particular tampon, they can try the next more absorbent one or use a liner to catch the overflow. Tampons should be changed every four hours, so girls should use pads when they are unable to replace tampons frequently. Tampons may work well during the day, while pads are better at night.

Girls should not practice using tampons at any other time than during their menstrual cycle. Tampons are absorbent and will absorb the normal vaginal secretions and potentially cause excessive dryness and irritation to the vagina.

Parents should review with their daughters the correct way of disposing of sanitary pads and tampons.

Toxic Shock Syndrome
A note of caution. A very rare but dangerous condition associated with the use of tampons is called *toxic shock syn-*

drome (TSS). If, while using tampons, you or your daughter develop fever, vomiting, diarrhea, and a skin rash, remove the tampon and see your physician. The absorbency of tampons disturbs the normal protective lining of the vagina. When that protection is disrupted, bacteria can enter the body and cause illness. Presently the tampons available on the market are less absorbent, and the risk of TSS is very low. Check the insert in the box of tampons for more information.

Menstruation: Commonly Asked Questions from Preadolescents and Parents

"Does it hurt to have a period?"

"Many young girls don't experience much discomfort when they first start having their periods. This may be because they are not ovulating yet. Ovulating is when an egg cell matures and leaves the ovary. But even though a girl may not be ovulating, the cycle continues, and she does have a period. Later on, though, as a girl's body becomes more regulated, ovulation occurs and periods can be uncomfortable. The uterus is a muscle that contracts in order to shed the built-up lining. These contractions are the cramps that you might feel during the first or second day of your period.

Fortunately, there are some simple things that can help ease cramps.

- Keep active. Mild exercise will help you feel invigorated and relieve some of the cramps.
- A warm shower or hot-water bottle can relax your muscles.
- Some medications such as ibuprofen or aspirin can help too.
- Be kind to yourself. Remember, having your period means your body is working well and is doing what it's supposed to.
- If none of these things help, we can ask the doctor for help."

"What kinds of things affect my period?"

"Many times, girls may stop having their periods, such as when they have a prolonged illness, play strenuous sports, or take dance training. Once the activity stops and the body re-adjusts, their period should start up again. And if you ever stop having your period and are worried, we can consult the doctor."

"When do periods stop?"

"As long as there are egg cells in the ovaries, the menstrual cycle occurs. Eventually all the available egg cells have matured, and along with hormonal changes in the woman's body, menstrual cycles stop. For most women, this occurs when they're around forty-five to fifty-five. This period in a woman's life is called *menopause.* Also, during pregnancy, the female body stops having periods because the uterine lining must be conserved to nourish the developing fetus."

"Can a tampon get lost in the body?"

"Sometimes, young girls think of their vagina as a dark, bottomless pit, and worry that if they insert tampons there, it might disappear into their body cavities and be lost forever. But you shouldn't worry about that. The opening to the uterus, the cervix, is very small and doesn't allow the tampon to get lost. There is no way that this can happen. Always remember, though, to remove the last tampon at the end of your period."

"How can I help my daughter feel more comfortable about using tampons?"

"There is no easy way of accomplishing this. Many girls this age would die before allowing their mothers to show them or help them with the insertion of a tampon. Nevertheless, your attitude toward your daughter's use of tampons is the more reliable indicator of whether she will be willing to try them or not. Girls should be encouraged to get to know their bodies. Using a mirror, with clean hands and in the privacy of their rooms, girls can look at their genitals and see where the vaginal opening is. The angle of the vagina can vary from one girl to the next. Using her finger to locate this angle is often very helpful. There is a sheet of instructions inside the tampon package that describes how to insert a tampon. Refer to these directions to learn the correct angle of insertion."

"When should a girl have a PAP smear and what exactly is it?"

"There usually is no need for a girl to have a PAP smear before age eighteen if she is not sexually active. All girls should have a PAP smear within one year of becoming sexually active. A PAP smear can be done by a general physician, gynecologist, or nurse practitioner. PAP stands for Papanicolaou, the name of the person who developed the technique. A PAP smear is a method of identifying cancer of the cervix."

16

****

ERECTIONS AND
WET DREAMS

I n order to better define the changes that occur during the
normal development of male sex characteristics between
prepuberty and adulthood, these changes have been di-
vided into five stages. Let's review them.

Stage 1—This is the prepubertal stage, the time from
birth until the beginning of puberty. Boys' genitals
grow along with the rest of the body, but growth is not
very noticeable.

Stage 2—This stage marks the beginning of puberty. The
main growth during this time is the enlargement of
the testes and the scrotum. With the growth of the testes, the scrotum also enlarges to accommodate them.
The color of the skin of the scrotum may also get
darker.

Stage 3—During this stage, the penis begins to grow. It
gets longer and wider. The testicles continue enlarg-
ing, and the scrotum darkens a bit more. By now, boys
notice the growth of pubic hair, and they also may discover that one testicle hangs a bit lower than the other.
This happens in order to prevent them from being
crushed against each other as males walk. The testicles
are extremely sensitive to trauma. All of these changes
are very normal.

Stage 4—A natural progression of growth continues throughout this stage. Additional pubic hair grows now in the typical, adult male distribution pattern of a diamond with the base at the penis and hairs up to the belly button. Pubic hairs become more abundant, coarse, and darker. They may also grow along the inner thighs and around the anus.

Stage 5—This is the adult stage. The penis is fully grown and is usually between two-and-a-half and four inches long when flaccid or soft. The testes have reached full-size, with one hanging a bit lower than the other. One is slightly larger than the other. The scrotum is darker. The pubic hair is darker and more coarse.

The timing of these changes can vary considerably among individuals. The changes from the beginning of puberty (Stage 2) until full adult growth (Stage 5), can take from two to six years. Pubertal development is all predetermined by the body's genetic timetable and, therefore, is specific for each individual. Reassuring your son that all these changes will occur at the right time and in the right sequence is the most important role parents can play.

Unlike girls, who are born with all their eggs cells, boys are not born with sperm cells. During puberty, various hormones, including the most common, *testosterone,* influence boys' bodies to produce sperm. The production of sperm takes place in the testicles. This is why growth of testicles is the first sign of puberty for boys. Once boys start producing sperm, they continue to do so for the rest of their lives. The body also produces other fluids that mix with the sperm. This mixture of fluids and sperm is called semen. The semen leaves the body during an ejaculation through the urethra. The urine also is

71

eliminated from the body through the urethra, but never at the same time as semen.

Erections

Babies in utero, infants, and young boys experience erections. The erection occurs as blood rushes to the penis. During an erection, the penis gets hard and stands out, or is erect. It may produce a bulge in the crotch area. Boys cannot always control whether or not they will have an erection, and during the early stages of puberty, spontaneous erections are very common. Furthermore, they are not necessarily associated with sexual thoughts. Erections can occur at any time and under different circumstances. For most boys, this unpredictability is the most embarrassing and awkward aspect of puberty. Young boys will benefit by being reassured that, for the most part, an erection is noticeable only to them. Many have figured out different ways to deal with an unpredictable erection. Some remain seated, cross or uncross their legs, or hold a book casually in front of themselves. The erection goes quickly. It usually takes only a minute or two. It is not necessary to have an ejaculation in order to end an erection, but often ejaculation occurs along with an *orgasm*. An orgasm is a series of pleasurable contractions centered in the genital area. For boys, an orgasm usually occurs with ejaculation. Only rarely will a youngster have an orgasm without ejaculating. During orgasm, the penis experiences a series of contractions that help spurt out the semen, and then it becomes soft again. Orgasms can occur during sexual intercourse or during many forms of sexual stimulation. (See Key 32 for a discussion of masturbation.)

Wet Dreams

Once the male body starts producing sperm, a boy may experience his first nocturnal emission, also known as a *wet dream*. This is an involuntary ejaculation that occurs only during sleep (including nap time), and is not necessarily associated with sexual thoughts. Most boys do experience wet dreams, and they are entirely normal. The amount of semen released is about one teaspoon.

For boys, experiencing wet dreams can be confusing if you have not prepared them. Their most common misinterpretation of this entirely normal event is that somehow they have wet their beds, or, worse yet, that something is terribly wrong with them. Be assured that your son, as he enters Stage 2, has a heightened awareness of and sensitivity to the bodily changes he is experiencing. He notes every minute development and measures it against what he knows is supposed to happen in order to verify whether or not he is normal. As parents, you can make sure that your son's fund of knowledge is accurate and is not grounded in the myths of his peers. It is normal for him to be fascinated by the changes in his body. He need not feel frightened by them if you provide counseling, books he can read in private, and the reassurance he needs to ensure his comfort with his own body.

Many boys first experience wet dreams around age fourteen, between Stages 2 and 3, so a number of other sexual changes have already occurred. Once a boy starts ejaculating, either involuntarily through wet dreams, or as a result of masturbation, he is potentially fertile and could father a child during sexual intercourse. Parents should be sure their sons know this.

Preventive Care

Circumcision is a procedure during which the fold of skin around the glans of the penis, called the foreskin, is removed. In our society many boys are circumcised and others are not. Either way, the penis feels and works the same.

In the uncircumcised boy, the foreskin may or may not be pulled back (retracted) easily. Under no circumstances should

Figure 16.1
The circumcised and uncircumcised penis

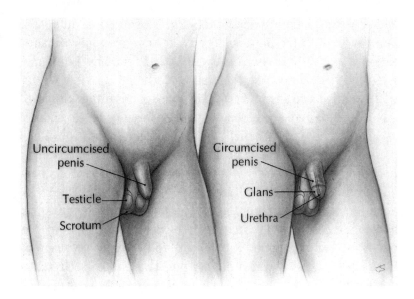

it be retracted forcefully. This may cause pain and could require medical attention. In some uncircumcised boys, the foreskin may not retract completely until age five or not until adolescence.

At puberty, the hygiene of the uncircumcised penis should be part of a young boy's routine, like shampooing hair or brushing teeth. A normal, oily substance, called smegma, accumulates on the inside of the foreskin and should be cleansed regularly. Boys need to learn to gently pull back the foreskin and clean this area on a regular basis.

Young teenagers also should learn testicular self-examination. This is a preventive measure during which the youngster examines his testicles for signs of cancer. A physician can provide instruction to your youngster about how to do this simple examination and what to look for. Basically, if there is any swelling in the groin area, lumps felt on the testicles, or sudden change in size of the testicles, contact your physician. By age fifteen, teens should practice testicular self-examination.

Commonly Asked Questions by Preteen Boys and Appropriate Parental Answers

"What if my penis is smaller than some of the other guys?"

"Boys worry about the size of the penis just like girls worry about the size of their breasts. The size of your penis has nothing to do with being a good athlete, how manly you are, or whether you'll have a satisfying future sexual life. Most adults' penises are about the same size and shape."

"When can I start to shave?"

"Are you excited about shaving? Some boys are and want to start as soon as the first fuzz appears on their faces. Probably you won't have facial hair until later during puberty. Remember that once you start, you'll continue doing it for the rest of your life. Shaving can be a real drag! Or, you may also decide not to shave and grow a beard. The amount of hair that you'll develop depends on inherited family characteristics. Grandpa has a thick, gray beard, but I have [Dad has] very little facial hair. The amount of facial and body hair you develop has nothing to do with your masculinity."

17

MOOD SWINGS

"As a parent, how do I deal with my preteen's emotional ups and downs so as make life easier for both of us?"

Of all the changes that take place during the preteen years, mood swings cause the most distress for parents. Preteens often feel and act grumpy and unhappy one minute and are semi-reasonable and cheerful the next. What was once a fond, close relationship between parent and child may turn into a tense, distant one. Friction, lots of eye rolling, and never-ending back talk are all associated with this stage of development. Preteens may not seem to need your approval anymore, and they appear to be very content doing things their own way, even if it is obvious that your way is better. Girls tend to express their emotions outwardly. Life becomes a daily drama, unfolding unevenly, with minor issues taking on major importance. Boys mature a year or two later than girls, and their mood swings are less dramatic during the preteens, but explode in their teenage years. It is generally believed that these mood swings are related to the hormonal changes that occur in the preteen's body, although this part of adolescence is not very well understood.

Of course, some youngsters breeze through this stage without conflict, but the majority experience some ambivalence about their transforming bodies and ever-changing feelings. Some youngsters have giggling fits that make parents feel a sense of awe at the degree of silliness displayed. The truth is that there probably is no easy way to prevent mood swings;

but your awareness that they are normal for preteen kids makes them more tolerable. Realizing that most preteens go through this stage—and come out intact—should be reassuring.

It is important when dealing with mood swings not to take comments, gestures, and smirks personally. For parents, this, too, is a time of uncertainty. What happened to my loving, sweet, happy, little child of yesterday? How do I deal with this volatile, sullen, crabby, cheerful chameleon? Parents who are tolerant of their children's ups-and-downs are better able to keep the channels of communication open. If your own self-worth is wrapped up in your youngster's opinion of you, you may be in for disappointment, because some days he or she apparently will not like you very much. Nevertheless, this *is* a time to remain involved in your child's life and *is not* the occasion to jump from the lifeboat. Moody and uncooperative may be the tone of the hour, but parents need to remain ever present in their youngster's life, to set guidelines and limits and to offer support.

When dealing with moody preteens, keep in mind the following points:

- Don't take their mood swings personally. As confusing as their behavior may be, try to understand that preteens are far more confused about their changing bodies and emotions than they will admit. It is safe for them to lash out at you, knowing that they have your unconditional love. It is a back-handed compliment.
- Wait for the storm to blow over. Then try to reestablish communication with your child when he or she seems more receptive. It may be easier to initiate conversation about a neutral subject before easing into a review of the feelings behind the last outburst. Perhaps when the cloud passes, you and

77

your youngster will be able to share a warm moment that will give you both hope for a better tomorrow.

- A helpful, nonthreatening phrase to use during a preteen's outburst is: "I don't talk to you in that manner; please don't talk to me that way." This, of course, requires great restraint on your part. If you lose control and yell back, the exchange will escalate to war status before it falls apart completely. At the same time, it is important to let your youngsters know that you are still in charge and in control of yourself in spite of what they may be going through. Be calm, even if you do not feel calm.

- There is nothing as valuable to confused preteens as having unconditional acceptance from the people who are still the most important ones in their lives: their parents. Showing your acceptance by spending time with your preteens is very important. But you do no favors for your children by suggesting magnanimously that you do things together that you like better than your preteens do. In this case, they feel like they are indulging *you*. Put aside the notion that you can decide what activities your children should enjoy, and take time to ferret out what things *they* like to do. Then spend time with them doing those things. Even watching their favorite TV program in silence, or a movie that rates no stars with you, can convey your acceptance of them and your availability, should they want to talk.

- Reassure your preteen that moods are feelings that, with time, will pass and may or may not recur. With time, these mood swings ease and youngsters can learn more efficient ways to deal with them, such as paying attention to their diet, exercising, deep breathing, or other forms of relaxation.

- Start teaching girls to observe and note mood changes associated with their menstrual cycles so they begin to understand and learn about their own cyclic patterns.

18

‸‸‸

SEXUAL IDENTITY AND ORIENTATION

Sexual identity can be defined as the image of the self as a male or female, plus the attitudes and beliefs about what being a male or female means. Sexual identity has three basic components: core identity, gender behavior, and sexual orientation.

Core identity refers to a person's gender at birth: male or female. This core identity is your child's inner sense of belonging to one gender or the other. Between the ages of eighteen months and three years, children begin to develop a sense of their own gender identity, a sense of being male or female. The concept that every human being is born one sex or the other, simple as it sounds from an adult's point-of-view, is reassuring to a young child who is beginning to struggle with the concepts of identity and differences between genders. It is not unreasonable to reinforce the basic concept that, yes, baby boys grow up into men, and baby girls into women.

Gender behavior refers to behavioral characteristics a particular culture expects each of its members to exhibit, based upon gender. Traditionally, society identifies certain behaviors as male and other behaviors as female. For example, in our society, we expect girls to be polite and quiet in their play. On the other hand, we assume that boys are more active and less sensitive to others' feelings. Societal changes occur over decades, resulting in reworked gender expectations. For instance, today both men and women work at jobs that once were held by only one gender or the other. As parents, you can help your children by allowing them to experience life without restrictions based upon their genders. Girls can be active, noisy, and have both male and female friends. Boys can be sensitive and enjoy quiet time alone. Both can grow up to be doctors or nurses, gardeners, chefs, engineers, or firefighters.

Sexual orientation refers to a persistent pattern of attraction to a person of the same or opposite sex. A person's sexual orientation can be heterosexual, homosexual, or bisexual. A heterosexual person is primarily attracted to or has romantic feelings toward a person of the opposite sex. A bisexual person is attracted to both men and women. A homosexual person (a gay man or lesbian woman) is attracted to a person of the same sex. In our society, the majority of people are heterosexual. It is believed that approximately 10 percent of the population are gay or lesbian. Some theories describe an individual's sexual orientation as part of a continuum in which he or she can be predominantly hetero- or homosexual or anywhere along the spectrum between the two.

Sexual orientation is not a choice and neither is it the result of a particular parenting style. It is important for parents to understand that a child's sexual orientation is predetermined and not decided or changed by parenting or societal influences. Neither can a person's sexual orientation be altered with therapy or medicine. An attraction to a person of the same sex is not a feeling one chooses. There are theories about the genetic mechanism that determines an individual's sexual orientation, but there is still a great deal to learn. A person's sexual orientation is only one, albeit important, part of the whole person. In every other way, gay males, lesbians, bisexuals, and heterosexuals are no more different than anyone else.

It is not unusual for children between the ages of eight and ten to have intense relationships with friends of the same sex. This is part of the normal developmental process and has no future impact upon a child's sexual orientation. The orientation is there from birth.

Explaining Sexual Orientation to Children

Between the ages of five and eight, children will be exposed to countless messages about sexual identity and orientation from the media, TV, school, and religious institutions. The media is a particularly insidious source of information because of its constant presence on the screens in our living rooms. Where you live (city/country, North/South), can affect the nature and the amount of TV coverage of sexually sensitive issues. No matter how carefully you monitor input, your children will hear crude terms, will absorb attitudes that do not reflect your family's values, and will be curious about alternative points-of-view. It is a parent's huge responsibility to interpret the volatile information that, if left alone, may leave our children with views about sexual identity that we feel are not healthy, kind, or accurate.

When talking to children from ages five to eight about sexual identity, you may want to start with a brief explanation of the different types of love that human beings are capable of experiencing. As adults, we know that the love we feel for children is different from the love we feel for spouses; and that is still different from the love we may feel for nature and humanity as a whole. When talking with your children about different types of love, key phrases to include are:

- There are different kinds of love that people experience.
- The love we parents feel for you children is different from the type of love Dad and I (Mom and I) feel for each other.

- Certain special feelings toward someone else are known as *sexual attraction.* When we have romantic feelings for that person, we get excited. These are good feelings.

As children get older, ages nine through twelve, they are able to understand the concept of sexual attraction better, although they are still not ready to comprehend fully the magnitude of it. This is the stage when everyone of the opposite sex is "yucky" and strong friendships abound among same-gender friends. Boys and girls tease each other at school if same-sex friends show any hint of attraction toward someone of the opposite sex. Boys at this age tend to segregate and play exclusively with groups of other boys. Girls tend to have one or two close friends with whom they spend their time.

Name calling is common among youngsters in this age group. Cruel names like *faggot, queer, dyke,* and *sissy* are insulting, offensive, and hurtful. It is crucial that parents instruct their children about how wrong it is to label people in derogatory ways based upon their sexual identities.

Talking to nine- to twelve-year-olds about sexual orientation should include the following key points:

- Men who are gay have sexual feelings and fall in love with other men. Homosexual men are also called *gay.*
- Women who are homosexual have sexual feelings and fall in love with other women. Homosexual women are known as *lesbians.*
- Homosexual people can have loving and caring relationships just like heterosexuals. They have romantic love for someone of the same sex rather than the opposite sex.
- Gay men and lesbians in committed relationships can form families by adopting children or by having their own children.

19

RITES OF PASSAGE

R ites of passage are ceremonies a society observes to celebrate the passage of its young individuals into a new stage of adult life. Different cultures celebrate these rituals in a variety of ways. Some are religious, such as the bar mitzvah and bat mitzvah for Jewish boys and girls respectively. Others are not. The American Indian Navajo tribes celebrate Kinaaldá, a coming-of-age ceremony, to honor their young girls. A long day of preparation, including cooking and an endurance run by the pubescent girl, marks the occasion.

Our culture, as a whole, could benefit from rites of passage for all young girls and boys. For instance, most adult women remember their first menstrual cycle with mixed emotions. Although our society does not laud this step into womanhood, menarche should be celebrated. Boys also deserve celebration as they enter puberty. Voices change, wet dreams occur, and shaving becomes part of a daily routine. For them, the changes associated with puberty are more subtle, less evident. Nevertheless, it is just as important to mark this passage for boys as it is for girls. Rites of passage for adolescents are ways of letting them know that puberty marks new and special milestones in their sexual development and self-definition. Of course, rites of passage need not celebrate puberty. (Though, why not?) A rite of passage can celebrate any other important "crossing" that is agreed upon by the youngster and his or her family. The point is to commemorate growth and development as events to be treasured and celebrated. We should honor our children by incorporating rites of passage into our culture!

While conducting classes for mothers and daughters about puberty, I asked mothers to share their thoughts and ideas about possible celebrations of rites of passage for young people entering puberty. How could we observe this transition and make it a memorable event for our children?

For most mothers this was a new concept. Yet, some were already planning for the event. As we brainstormed together, many ideas emerged about when or what should mark the celebration, or rite of passage. Some mothers felt the beginning of the menstrual cycle was the most important occasion for daughters. Others felt a particular age should be cause for celebration. Still others believed their children should choose their own occasion for a rite of passage. The following suggestions were made as to how to celebrate a child's passage:

- A whole day spent together (mother and daughter or father and son) doing activities they both enjoy.
- Perhaps celebrating by buying a special token of adulthood. It might be a book, a piece of jewelry, or a more grown-up piece of clothing.
- A special letter and a grown-up gift from Mom and Dad.
- A special gift of a book about characters who experience passages into adulthood.
- Ceremonies honoring the young person. (See Suggested Readings for more information.)
- A special present of a family heirloom, presented with the stories behind it, explaining the importance of being its keeper.
- Getting a girl's ears pierced, or getting a boy a shaving kit.
- A teen party to celebrate.
- An overnight trip with just Mom or Dad.
- An evening with same sex relatives so they can relate stories from their own childhood.

- Have a formal family dinner. Each family member will give the youngster a fresh flower or other small token and tell a story that illustrates why he or she is special to them.
- Plan a special family dinner and evening well ahead of time. Ask your youngster what he or she wants to eat and do for the evening. Review the plans periodically to keep current. Do not keep the plan a secret from the rest of the family. They should look forward to it with the honoree.
- A family camping trip or an out-of-town ballgame.
- Learning a new family activity now that the youngster has entered puberty.
- Setting aside some extra space for personal music equipment or hobby.

Remember that a daughter's passage can be celebrated with her father as well as with her mother and a son's with his mother, too. The celebration easily can include the whole family. A fourth-grade teacher told me that her father bought her a dozen roses and took her out to dinner when she started her menstruation. She remembers being a late-bloomer. As a happily married woman, she has never forgotten this kind gesture, and remembering it still brings tears to her eyes. To this date, she has a very close relationship with her father. What a special way to remember a father figure!

Whatever you do to celebrate your children's rites of passage depends on what is appropriate for them. The most important point is that parents acknowledge their children's "crossing" as they progress toward adulthood.

20

^^

FAMILY RELATIONSHIPS

N o single aspect of a child's life proves a more powerful influence in the development of sexuality than the family. It is within the family unit that children begin to establish a sense of identity, a value system, and models for future relationships. Here, too, children learn how to relate to others, how to give and receive affection, how to communicate effectively, and how to resolve conflicts. All of these skills contribute to your child's healthy sexuality and help ensure satisfying, adult relationships.

The family is the basic social unit of our society and reflects the diversity of today's culture. The result of this diversity is that the family unit often differs significantly from that of the traditional, nuclear one. Today's family may consist of a single household with one parent and one child, a parent and a stepparent, two mothers, two fathers, adoptive parents, grandparents, adopted or foster children, or a combination of these. It is important for children to understand that, regardless of their family's structure, they are closely joined with responsible adults who are there to love them, care for them, and meet their basic needs. Family relationships may change over the course of time, but the essence of family members taking care of and loving each other is a concept that should be a constant. The more parents nurture and validate family relationships, the more secure and valuable children feel. This takes parents' time, effort, and commitment.

In turn, it is important for children to see and understand that caring for a family is an enormous undertaking. The job requires quite a roster of people. It takes parents who are willing to invest the necessary time and energy to address family needs; it also takes caregivers in the persons of other family members and friends; and it requires children to run a smooth family operation. Youngsters should be encouraged to participate in the everyday chores, planning, and decision-making process in their families. When children are given clear roles to fill, and understand they are as important to the success of the family as the adults are, they will begin to develop a sense of value and pride in the importance of family and relationships in general.

Siblings

Siblings' interactions play important roles in how youngsters learn to develop healthy relationships. Families who have more than one child invariably are faced with sibling rivalry. Parents should be aware that rivalry is not a reflection of poor parenting skills. In fact, conflict among children within the same family is usual. Parents can play an important role by understanding and accepting skirmishes among their children and by learning different approaches to help youngsters deal with their brothers and sisters. Providing children with a forum in which to settle their differences with their siblings and to practice basic social skills is of utmost importance to their dealing successfully with future relationships. On a healthy, safe, practice ground, brothers and sisters can learn to negotiate and communicate effectively so that their relationships with one another, with friends, and with their future mates will all be enhanced. Often, shared information on sexuality can be very comforting to a preteen when it is reinforced by an older sibling.

Extended Family

Due to the increased transience of people in today's society, the extended family often is scattered geographically. Relatives are often no longer clustered within the same city or even the same state. Physical contact has been replaced by the telephone, mail, or telecommunication. Parents should lay the foundation for their children's closeness to significant others by demonstrating that *they* can and do take the time and effort to stay in touch with extended family members themselves. Nurturing these relationships underscores the value of family connections for children and provides them with a reassuring sense of belonging to a family culture with a widely spread and strong embrace.

Children enjoy seeing where they fit into the larger picture of their origins. What were their parents like when they were kids? And how were *they* parented? Who really walked five miles to school in blinding snowstorms? Parents should show their kids photographs from the past and tell stories about their own childhoods. Children especially feel good about similarities they share with their parents and grandparents. Parents can point these out through statements like, "Your grandpa liked to climb trees just like you do. He had long, strong legs, too." A strong sense of past in your children's present provides them with a greater sense of security.

Parents can ask other family members to serve as mentors and share family values related to sexuality with their children. Many times, these close extended family members can be role models and educators of sexuality to children who are uncomfortable speaking with their parents.

Preteens

Although the preteen youngster may need more personal and emotional space to grow, parents should be assured that, all evidence to the contrary, the family relationship is still important to the child. In fact, the importance of family involvement during these critical years is underestimated. Many youngsters are ambivalent about the process of separation as they approach their teens; although they may deny it, they count on seeing their parents at home, at school, and at sporting events. The lifeline, though frayed, is still quite strong between you and your children. Your preteens need the option to be included in all family activities, even though they often will choose to do "their own thing."

Adopted Family Members

Most children know a classmate, friend, or relative who is adopted. Most families with one or more adopted children have addressed adoption with their youngsters early and often. They are comfortable talking to their own children and others about this topic, and most are happy to be resources for other adoptive parents by suggesting ways to present information about adoption to both their adopted and biological children.

When talking to elementary-age children about adoption, the following phrases can be used.

- Sometimes a mother who is having a baby decides she cannot take care of her child. Because she wants the baby to have a good, happy life, she allows another couple who *can* take good care of the baby to be the baby's mom and dad. She lets them *adopt* the baby. It becomes their child.
- A woman who places her baby for adoption usually is young and does not have enough money to buy what the baby needs.

89

- Placing a baby for adoption can be a very painful decision for the mother and father who are giving their baby up.
- Many women are happy to know that their babies will be cared for and loved by another family who really want a baby and can take good care of it.
- There are different ways to adopt a baby. Certain people know how to help a pregnant woman find the best home for her baby. And people who want a baby can go to those people for help, too.
- Children who are adopted become loved members of their new families just like the other people in the family.
- We feel the same excitement within the family about adopting a new baby as we feel about having a baby ourselves. The result in both cases is a brand new member of the family.

Key Points for Establishing Healthy
Family Relationships

- Stay in touch and share with family members and close friends. The effort and commitment you invest in these relationships serve as examples for your child's future relationships, too.
- Display pictures of past and present family members.
- Talk about family origins.
- Cultivate family traditions and rituals that occur on a regular basis, such as holidays, birthdays, and other secular and religious occasions. Make them important.
- Learn ways to help siblings deal with rivalry in a healthy manner.
- Show acceptance of the diversity of family units in our present society, including adoptive families, stepparented families, single-parent families, and so forth. It is most important that commitment and a sense of caring for the children exist in your family, regardless of the parental structure.

- Spend time reading stories with children or, even better, telling stories about your own past.
- Include children in the family chores according to their abilities and ages.

The personal and interpersonal skills that are required to navigate the adult world are cultivated in the way family members interact with each other. Establishing healthy relationships during children's early years can enhance their ability to learn and practice the necessary skills for gaining and maintaining important alliances as they grow older. Certainly, learning how to be in relationships is an essential component of human sexuality and is indispensable when seeking a lifelong mate.

21

~~~~~~

THE SINGLE FATHER

With the increasing number of divorces and subsequent blended families in our society, many single fathers find themselves having to take active roles in the sexual education of their children, without the support of spouses. This situation can concern those parents who will deal with an opposite-sex child: father with daughter, and mother with son. In cases where both parents, though divorced, will play active roles in the sexual education of their children, conflicts still arise about which parent should be responsible for teaching what, when, and how. In addition, if a stepparent enters into the family portrait, the role of that person in the stepchild's sexual education must be clarified.

The Single Father and Daughter

If there has been a good father-daughter relationship before a divorce that grants joint custody or sole custody to the mother, in spite of difficult visitation constraints, a daughter's continuing relationship with her father should be encouraged. She should be able to count on her father to foster her assertiveness and to guide her in both important and unimportant matters. This guidance can be expressed best through a dad's continued and regular involvement regularly in his daughter's life. The way a father treats his daughter is the yardstick she eventually will use as a standard to measure other men in her life. In addition, seeing how her father treats her mother, before and after divorce, sets the guidelines for how she will expect other men to treat her, too. An involved and steady nearness in his daughter's life is one way a father can ensure the presence of a good male-model for her.

A father's advice and guidance is valuable in countless areas of his daughter's life, but it is valid to say that many preteen girls will be more comfortable having a detailed discussion about menstruation with their mothers than with their fathers. A father should check with his daughter to see if she has a preference. If she prefers female council and a mother is not available, a father may recruit another female family member, or ask a stepmother to address this sensitive subject. This specified female should discuss menstruation with the daughter on a one-to-one basis. A father can also see that there are books about menstruation available in his home for his daughter to read. He should maintain a supply of sanitary napkins or tampons (depending upon a daughter's preference), and it is helpful for divorced parents to communicate with one another about their daughter's needs so that a combined supply of products will be available whenever and wherever their child is with each of them.

Divorced fathers must be aware of the need for privacy that emerges during preadolescence. Most girls want and require their own space in their bedrooms and bathrooms, and this solitude should not be viewed by the parent as a sign of rejection. This urge for privacy is of utmost importance to the preteen girl, and cannot be overstated. Fathers must be flexible in this father-daughter relationship so as to allow the separation that naturally occurs as girls enter their adolescent years.

A supportive, divorced father can have a lasting impact on his daughter's self-esteem, just as he did before the divorce. During the pre- and adolescent years, he can serve as a buffer when there is friction between mother and daughter if the two ex-spouses are able to put their personal feelings aside and work for what is in their child's best interest.

The Single Father and Son

The single (or divorced) father and son may seem like a more natural, comfortable combination for discussing sexuality, but this is not necessarily so. Without thorough knowledge, fathers, too, will be uncomfortable dealing with the multiple themes of sexuality as they speak with their sons. Furthermore, many fathers are equally reluctant to seek outside help for this sensitive area. Fathers *can* and *should* play vital roles in teaching their sons, but *must* enhance their own education in the fields of sexuality and child development first. An uninformed dad may cover his lack of knowledge and comfort by making fun of sexuality through superficial or inappropriate comments and jokes. Youngsters, sensing a parent's awkwardness, shy away from asking questions about what they do not know. Fathers may vaguely remember their own awkward introduction to "the talk" or the lack of any sort of information shared at home and their struggle to acquire appropriate sexual information as they were growing up. Therefore, although the single father and son relationship may seem the most natural, it can perpetuate misconceptions and misinformation among boys if the single father does not make the effort to present sexuality in an informed, positive, healthy, and open light.

Single, divorced, or widowed fathers can be powerful models for their sons when they deal with female relationships. Each time a son sees his father interact with a female, for any reason, he perceives messages about what is appropriate behavior in relating to the opposite sex. Whatever code the parent describes through his words and actions, the son is likely to emulate. Seeing his father share, communicate, and live his life using strong, clear principles, is a gift every son should receive.

Key Points for the Single Father and His Children

- Take the initiative in talking with your children about sexual issues. Start with a general approach to the topic and observe your child's level of comfort. Use this barometer to guide you further. Perhaps you will need to solicit help from books, other family members, or same-sex friends.
- Respect your child's sense of privacy.
- Try to put differences with your ex-wife aside when dealing with child-related issues.
- Have appropriate reading material available such as picture books, brochures, or other literature about sexual health. Keep your child's developmental level in mind. (See Suggested Readings.)
- Not only avoid making fun or teasing your youngsters about the changes that they may be going through, but openly admire their growth and new levels of maturity.
- Find role models who can talk to and mentor preteen children. These can be teachers at school, family friends, coaches, or other community members you admire and respect.
- Do not share your current personal, sexual turmoil with your children. But children love hearing about parents' ups-and-downs during their own puberty.

There is no reason fathers should feel reluctant to take active roles in their children's sexual education. All parents need to take their clues from their children about when to advance, back up, or choose a different course. Even if your preteen does not eagerly approach you for information, keep the lines of communication open so that your child will be encouraged to come to you in the future with questions about the moral issues around sexuality.

22

^^

THE SINGLE
MOTHER

I n our society, it is usually the mother who addresses the topic of sexuality with children. Regardless of marital status, or the sex of the children, mothers most often assume the role of sexual educator.

While studies suggest mothers spend more time in direct communication with their children than fathers do, addressing sexuality still causes uneasiness for some moms. Presently, recognizing that sexuality is a vital part of their youngsters' education, more and more single mothers search for information that will help them address this important aspect of child rearing.

The Single Mother and Son

In our present society, the number of single mothers raising sons is growing at an unprecedented rate. More than one-third of households are headed by single mothers. Necessity demands, therefore, that these women take a proactive role in their sons' sexual educations.

A single mother should begin by studying basic information about the normal bodily changes her son will experience during puberty. She may also want to review female transitions so she will be able to share this knowledge with her son as well. Most mothers find it is easier to speak about menstruation to their sons than to talk to them about wet dreams. Nevertheless, armed with sufficient knowledge, a mom should not allow fear to prevent either of these discussions.

Occasional educational opportunities for mother-son classes are slowly emerging in local communities through churches and organizations such as Planned Parenthood to address the needs of single mothers and their sons. These classes are usually directed by male role models and serve to break the ice and open up discussions between mothers and sons about sexuality. Such courses help to de-mystify the topic of human sexuality for both, and prepare mothers to be viable sources of further information as their sons need it. Mothers who take this step of commitment to their son's sexual education should be commended.

Mothers who may find this role as sexual educator uncomfortable, can enlist family members, role models from the community, Big Brothers, or male friends to mentor their sons. Certainly, a combination of mother and mentor can work as well. Obviously, trusted advisors should be chosen who will reflect the mother's values and will serve as strong role models.

The Single Mother and Daughter

Several roadblocks may interrupt the smooth transfer of knowledge between the single mother and her child. Problems arise when mothers do not pick up on their daughters' embarrassment or when they fail to remember that children under stress sometimes cannot formulate clear questions. At other times, a daughter senses her mother's apprehension and, in order to spare her any further discomfort, takes on the adult role of protecting the mom by avoiding the subject of sexuality altogether.

Many mothers are eager to talk with their daughters about sexuality, but hesitate, fearing that they will say too much, will not understand important concepts well enough to speak clearly about them, or will feel embarrassed by a daughter's explicit questions. All of these are valid, normal concerns, but they should not impede mothers from forging ahead. By talking with other mothers of preteen daughters, single moms can see how normal their own fears and concerns are. For all parents, finding the balance between providing information that keeps their children safe and healthy, without burdening them with fear about future sexual decisions, is a delicate challenge. There are no easy routes to success, and trial and error are parts of every normal journey. Single mothers must struggle with both the words they use and their attitudes about their own sexuality as they work to impart a healthy, lifelong perspective of sexuality to their daughters.

Key Points for the Single Mother and Her Children

- Be proactive when dealing with sexual issues. Plan your responses to those anticipated questions that may make you feel uncomfortable. Practice your responses with close friends, family members, or alone in front of a mirror.
- Respect your child's sense of privacy, particularly that of the opposite-sex child.
- Have reading material, picture books, and brochures about sexual health available for your children that is appropriate to their developmental age. (See Suggested Readings.)
- Use teachable moments such as TV viewing or current events to discuss your values and beliefs about sexuality.
- Avoid making fun of or teasing your child as his or her bodily changes begin to occur.
- Find role models who can talk to and mentor your child, especially during the early and mid-adolescent years. These can be family members, friends, or community and church members you admire and respect.
- Remain involved in the religion or belief of your choice. Sexuality is closely linked to values, morals, and a code of ethics

that can be solidified within the context of belonging to and believing in a greater picture of life.

- Do not share your personal sexual turmoil with your children. Whether you are divorced or not, there are aspects of a parent's adult life that should remain private.
- Celebrate changes in your child as milestones are reached. (See Rites of Passage, Key 19.)

The single-parent family is common in today's society. The causes are several. Death and divorce are the most usual, though single people elect parenthood as well. In all cases, the security of each affected child will diminish or flourish depending upon a parent's commitment to their healthy upbringing. In all cases, when parents commit to their child's sexual education, they must struggle both with the words they use and with their own attitudes about sexuality as they convey information that will help ensure their youngster's healthy future.

23

▲▲

FRIENDSHIPS, CRUSHES, AND PEER PRESSURE

T he concept of friendship develops at a very early age and is a keystone for future relationships. Learning the skills to make, keep, and end friendships will benefit your children for the rest of their lives.

Friendships

Parents can help children develop friendship skills by providing children with the opportunities to play and interact with other children their own age. As children grow, gender-based differences in their play are identifiable. Boys tend to interact in larger groups, select other boys to play with, and are rougher. Girls are apt to play with one or two other girls, share secrets. Both act out imaginary roles. Although clear gender differences exist, even at very young ages, there is value in reinforcing that boys and girls can be friends in spite of them.

Even between the best of friends, arguments and name calling occurs. Parents can use teachable moments to help resolve skirmishes and to direct their offspring away from making hurtful comments. Parents or caregivers also should serve as role models, using appropriate language when dealing with their own anger during conflicts and encouraging children to follow their lead.

As your child enters primary school, playmates become more self-selected. Girls play mostly with girls, and boys with boys. This trend of same-sex friendship continues well into the preadolescent years. Parents can learn a great deal about their children by paying close attention to their friends. With whom do they like to play? How do they interact? Are they aggressive? Submissive? Although children should be allowed to resolve their own conflicts within friendships, parents should be watchful for conflicts caused by name calling, disproportionate power struggles, or blatantly unkind behavior. It is appropriate for a parent to intervene if interaction among youngsters feels or looks uncomfortable to you. For example, you could say, "Let's use words to tell Jimmy how you are feeling about not getting a chance to play with the train." Then, after Jimmy expresses himself and the issue is resolved, a peaceful period ensues. Parents now can praise the children's behavior. "The two of you are playing so nicely. What good friends!" Most of the time, though, parental intervention is not necessary since children will avoid uncomfortable relationships on their own. Parents, therefore, should respect the youngsters' choices of friendships, realizing that there may be underlying benefits in them that parents cannot see. Learning how to make and keep friendships takes practice, and there will surely be some ups-and-downs during the course of them.

Crushes

As children enter their preteen years, they may experience crushes on opposite or even same-sex individuals. The object of their desires may be peers, older classmates, movie or music stars, or teachers; no one is off limits. These often sexual, romantic feelings, directed toward the desired person, are all played out within a youngster's imagination, giving an opportunity to experience feelings without having to act upon them—in other words, without taking the risks associated with a relationship. It is a safe way of dealing with new emotions since it is extremely unlikely that the crush will ever manifest itself as a real relationship. Crushes can eventually lead to hurt feelings when reality steps in. For instance, when the beloved computer teacher marries during spring vacation, a young, silent suitor experiences disappointment. Nevertheless, crushes are part of pre- and adolescent growth and can be viewed as healthy.

Having a crush on someone of the same sex does not necessarily suggest anything about a youngster's sexual orientation. It is quite common for young boys to feel attracted to male figures although they may not admit these feelings to their friends, and certainly not to their parents. The same can occur when girls feel particularly attracted to female role models or to girlfriends. Again, this is not necessarily an indication of homosexuality. Both boys and girls can have crushes on same-sex individuals and go on to establish their individual sexual identities without difficulty. One of the characteristics of crushes is that they are transient. They resolve as quickly as they develop. In fact, a youngster can have ardent feelings for many individuals at the same time. The hope is, that as youngsters experience infatuations, they will experiment with romantic feelings without having to deal with the consequences or act upon those feelings. Later, when they revisit the now-familiar emotions they will have matured enough to act responsibly on them.

Peer Pressure

Peer pressure can start at an early age and never really ends. Although it is often viewed as negative, it does not have to be. Youngsters who spend time around other children with similar values can share positive influences and can reinforce exemplary behaviors, such as volunteerism and acceptance of people's differences.

As youngsters enter the preteen years, parents' levels of comfort increase when they see the enhanced capabilities of their children. This maturity goes hand-in-hand with the preteens' sudden surge in their need for independence. They begin to form strong attachments to same-sex friends and to explore many relationships. Secrets are shared, oaths of camaraderie are taken, and friendships come and go with amazing ease. During this time, peer pressure may gain a stronger foothold. In order to retain friendships and their own sense of belonging, youngsters often rely heavily on their peer groups for acceptance and validation. It is under these circumstances that peer pressure plays a role in preteens' decisions about drugs, alcohol, and sex-related, risk-taking behaviors.

Therefore, preteens need skills to help them critically evaluate the potential risks of behaviors that might appear tempting, such as shoplifting, drug and alcohol use, and engaging in early sex. Waiting until a child is already engaged in these activities to disarm negative, dangerous behavior is unsafe and much more difficult for parents than addressing potential problems. Parents should talk to their preteens about peer pressure and explore ways with them in which they can deal with potentially problematic situations. For example, parents and their youngsters can role-play various "what if . . ." scenarios. This is a technique that is invaluable in so many life situations that the earlier a youngster learns about it, the better. Those following are scenarios addressing peer pressure: What if . . .

- you and your best friend were at the mall, and she shoplifted an inexpensive item from the store. What would you do or say to her? How would her stealing make you feel? How would it affect your friendship with her?
- you are walking down the hall of school and you are approached by the most popular guy or girl, who offered you a

cigarette or drugs? If you accept you may be asked out on a date.

• your new boyfriend or girlfriend wants to hold hands all the time or kiss you in front of the entire school?

As preteens become teens, the "what if's . . ." become even more important. For example what if . . .

• your boyfriend or girlfriend and you are at a party and he or she gets drunk?
• you are at a school game and your friends are doing drugs?
• your best friend confides to you that a step-parent has made sexual overtures?

Parents can help youngsters think ahead and prepare responses to these and other similar situations. They also can teach their children simple, one-sentence responses to help them deal with peer pressure, such as,

• "Stealing is wrong."
• "No thanks. Drugs are not for me."
• "A real friend wouldn't push me to do something that's bad for me."
• "I am not ready for kissing."
• "Do not pressure me to do what I don't want to do."
• "Why is it important that other people see us kissing? I think kissing is private."
• "I am happy with myself just as I am. I don't need drugs."

Friendships are an important type of human relationship. Having friends and sharing with them provides great joy. It is through friendships that children can begin to understand human nature and, consequently, themselves. The skills that children learn for making and keeping friends as they grow up are no different from those needed to nurture and cultivate a committed, lifelong relationship.

24

~~~~~~

MARRIAGE, LIFETIME COMMITMENTS, AND DIVORCE

One of the more important decisions your child will make is choosing a lifetime mate. This crucial decision will be based in part on feelings of romantic love, but clear, rational thinking is essential for making a good choice as well. In order to select a partner, young people must first understand themselves well; they must have a distinct, strong value system that is nourished from early childhood; and they must determine some of their major goals for the future. Most experts agree that although opposites may attract, and often *do* marry, a relationship based on dissimilar points of view often does not work. When two people have similar tastes, values, religions, and dreams, there is a much better opportunity for a stable foundation upon which to build a happy marriage. Finding someone with these important similarities and goals to whom one is physically and mentally attracted as well, is the unearthing of one of life's greatest treasures.

The makeup of the family and the dynamics within each familial unit will have a lasting impact on the development of a child's sexuality. Children who live in homes with two parents can understand the significance of marriage or lifetime commitment when they see that their parents place a high value and priority on their own commitment to each other. They can note, through their parents' actions, that marriage takes time, energy, and dedication on behalf of two responsible adults who, in addition to sharing similar values, are physically attracted to one another. Although most men and women grow up and marry, not everyone does. Preteens can begin to comprehend that many gay men and lesbians live in committed relationships, even though these alliances may not be recognized by law. Preteens in single-parent families can also learn that adults can have fulfilling lives without being married.

For parents who want to advocate sexual abstinence for their young teens, stating your values about the institution of marriage or a similar lifelong commitment is essential. If you believe in abstinence before serious commitment you might tell your children what your values are and why this is valuable to you. (See Key 31 for further information on abstinence.) Reminding children often that sex is just one aspect of sexuality is important as well.

If one considers the inflating divorce rate in our society, it is easy for parents and their children to draw the conclusion that marriage is devalued. Certainly statistics suggest this. Over half of all marriages end in divorce and an increasing number of couples choose to live together outside the institution. At the same time, hope is offered through an increasing number of articles in popular magazines and newspapers that announce, "Marriage is making a comeback!"

Most parents, whether they have been divorced or not, would like to believe that their own children will grow up and find lifetime mates whom they can love forever. Divorced parents can be realistic, accepting that there is a tendency for children to repeat their parents' patterns. But they can be en-

106

couraging as well, promoting the concept of the great worth of selecting commitment to a loved one.

When parents go through a divorce, no matter how amicable the circumstances, the change is monumental for most children. From a child's perspective, the possibility that they somehow are responsible for their parents' divorce is almost always present. Similarly, they may fantasize that they can bring their moms and dads back together. These are normal feelings. With time they lessen, and acceptance eventually replaces the wish to reunite parents.

Children should be told matter-of-factly that they are not responsible for their parents' divorce. As with many other aspects of children's lives, this concept must be repeated many times in a variety of different circumstances. Children should be reassured also that parents divorce each other, not their kids. Professional help is available in most communities for both parents and children to help resolve inner feelings and cope with the break in the family circle.

Key Points about Teaching Children Basic Concepts of Marriage and Divorce

- Marriage is a legal contract/agreement between two responsible, committed adults who share values, dreams, responsibilities, and physical and mental attraction.
- A marriage takes work, time, and effort. It is a relationship that allows room for emotional growth and change in both persons involved.
- Children grow and are cared for by parents who are willing to take on the responsibilities of parenthood.
- Some people decide to live together without being married.
- Gay men and lesbian women live in lifelong, committed relationships even though their partnership may not be recognized as marriage.

- Most people hope to marry and to live in a committed, life-long relationship.
- Some couples may choose not to have children.
- Divorce is the legal ending of a marriage. Divorce can occur for a variety of different reasons.
- Divorce is an adult decision and not the responsibility of the children.
- When parents get divorced, they may choose to remarry or not.
- When parents divorce, the decisions about custody of children and financial resources may be decided by parents themselves or by lawyers and judges.
- Children, as well as the adults experiencing divorce, may need professional help to deal with their feelings.

Marriage and lifelong commitments take time to cultivate. When two responsible adults decide to spend their lives together, their decision should be based on maturity, love, and a commitment to one another.

25

^^

LOVE AND AFFECTION

L ove is a fundamental aspect of all close human relationships, so children must receive and experience love from their parents. Being cared for in a nurturing environment is the foundation upon which children's healthy sexuality will develop and flourish. Seeing how people give and receive affection, particularly parents and immediate family members, becomes mirrored in youngsters' minds for use in future relationships. It also provides them with unspoken guidelines for the ways people treat each other in general. Feeling loved moves people to do good, to care for others, and to live moral lives.

Love and Affection for the Preschooler

During the early preschool ages, children can learn that people show their love toward each other in a variety of ways. Love is having deep, warm feelings for oneself and for others. One way of sharing loving feelings is by telling those we love how we feel. Love can also be expressed by hugs, kisses, smiles, pats on the head, or by listening attentively while another is speaking. Children should learn to share affection with those closest to them: their family members, friends, daycare workers, teachers, and neighbors.

Another concept that preschool children begin to experience and comprehend is that, even when there is love between two people, there can be many emotional ups-and-downs.

They can see that parents and friends can be angry at each other and still love one another. They can also see that, when their parents are angry at them, they are still loved. Parents can and do feel anger at their kids, but they do not stop loving them. Anger and love can coexist. Understanding the differences among these feelings can start at a very early age and is invaluable to any child's emotional well-being.

Love and Affection for the Preteen

When children ask questions about love and sexuality, parents are given an open door to convey their family's values and, hopefully, to guide and mold their children's feelings and actions in loving relationships. Defining love is no easy task, and clearly there are many different types of love. There is love for parents and family members, for friends and relatives, for pets, for nature, and for the less fortunate. For future healthy relationships, children also need to realize that loving themselves is part of the whole picture.

The type of love that parents feel toward their children is an intimate love through which they share feelings, encouragement, and the desire to communicate with and support their children, while helping to meet their needs. This feeling of love is shared with those closest to us, and hopefully, will be present later in marriage or a committed relationship.

Preteens must learn that sexual attraction is very different from love. Sexual attraction is having and wanting to share intense sexual feelings with another person. It includes infatuation; it is feeling physically attracted to another person. Infatuation can include romantic and loving aspects as well as sexual ones. It is a wonderful feeling, but it is not the only one required to maintain a healthy relationship.

Because they are older, preteens also can understand more fully the concepts of committed love. They should know

110

this is the type of love that includes shared values and goals as well as friendship, romance, and sexuality, and that it does not always come easily. It occurs between adults who have decided they love each other, have shared vows of that love, and have declared that they will do whatever it takes to maintain their relationship. The two people entering this lasting relationship are dedicated to similar goals and are anxious and willing to share a life together, in spite of the obstacles that are part of every life. Children best understand this special love when they see consistent models of it in their environment. They learn that time and maturity are required to achieve it and that regular attention maintains it. Sadly, portraits of this sort of love are less and less available to youngsters.

Time-in for All Children

The ability to establish loving relationships is a cornerstone to a child's healthy sexuality. Parents have an opportunity to model the necessary skills by sharing time with their children. This habit will make sharing an important part of our kids' committed relationships later on. I cannot stress the concept of *time-in* enough. I guarantee it will enhance parents' relationships with their children if it is practiced consistently throughout their growing-up years.

Spending time with children may seem to be what most parents do on a daily basis by living with them. But time-in is really quite different. Time-in means spending time with your child, doing what he or she wants, according to his or her terms. A parent gives a child the opportunity to pick an activity (within reason, of course), and the parent assumes the role of follower as the activity is played out. The child should be the one in charge. During this time, there is ample opportunity to talk, share, or just be with the child on a one-to-one basis. The concept of time-in can expand in your child's life to enhance not just you and your youngster's relationship, but that between your child and any regular caretaker such as a favorite sitter or childcare provider. I would go so far as to recommend that this concept is one that, when utilized regularly, separates good daycare from mediocre.

As children get older, spending time with an individual parent, one-on-one, can occur over a meal. Many times, having a special activity that a parent and child can participate in is another way to enhance relationships. The activity should be repeated consistently, whether it is once a day, once a week, or, at the very least, once a month.

The concept of time-in is one parenting tool that works year after year as children grow into adults.

Key Points about Time-in

- Time-in should be provided on a regular basis regardless of a child's behavior before the appointed time.
- Time-in can be labeled as "Special Time" or "Andrew's Time."
- The child chooses the activity and is the leader.
- The parent chooses the time and is the follower. Start with a short time; ten to fifteen minutes may be sufficient. Use a timer.
- No interruptions. Let the answering machine get the calls, and make sure other family members understand the rules.
- No misbehavior should be allowed and if it does occur, the usual consequences should apply, and special time is shortened.

Having a loving relationship with our children can last a lifetime. Such a bond serves as a template for their future loving relationships. Here are some key points for parents to remember.

- Display your child's school accomplishments such as art, re-port cards, and anything that says: "We are proud of you, and you should be proud of yourself as well."
- Let your children know you love them unconditionally. All children need at least one person who is crazy about them. Grandparents, aunts, uncles, or other adults who spend time with the child are worthy additions.
- Talk to your children about different types of feelings. Label those feelings for them (mad, sad, glad, frustrated) as you see them experience them.
- Spend individual time with your child doing an activity that he or she enjoys. Make it a ritual that connects the two of you and that will become an important memory later on.

26

VALUES AND BELIEFS

V alues are qualities of the human personality that have an abiding worth; the norms by which a person lives his or her life, the ethics of what is right and wrong. A value can also be defined as a quality that benefits not only the one receiving the gain but also the one practicing the value. Parents want their children to grow up with a set of ethics that will sustain and nurture them as responsible individuals in our society. Some parents, though, may not have made the effort to determine what their own values are. In this case, *now* is the essential time to get your value system in order.

In a recent *Newsweek* poll, 48 percent of parents of children under four years responded that bringing up a moral child was their most important parental goal. Most parents agree that the code of behavior they want their children to learn includes honesty, courage, self-reliance and discipline, respect, kindness, and justice. Of course, there are many other values that may be particularly important in your family. These, too, should be added to your list.

A person's sense of right and wrong is molded by time and by the influence of family, friends, society, religion, and the media. Therefore, although many parents hope that children will grow up with a similar set of values to theirs, children may choose different ones to live their lives by because they are exposed to influences other than their parents'.

As children get older, their cognitive abilities allow them to think and reason more deeply as they begin to make their own choices about what constitutes ethical behavior. There is a window of opportunity between ages nine and eleven to talk to children about moral choices. The opening occurs when youngsters are old enough to comprehend larger concepts and still have close relationships with their parents. During this period, parents can and should convey their values about sexuality that will influence their children's lives for the better later on.

Teaching Values

There are various ways of exposing children to appropriate conduct, and, essentially, teaching them good principles is no different from instructing them in math, hygiene, cooking, or sexuality. Parents can use frequent repetition, teachable moments, and can set their own good examples. They can take a proactive stance and provide value training to children as opportunities arise during everyday activities. Preschool children learn about right and wrong through example and copious praise when their own behavior reflects proper conduct. The preteen youngster learns from factual information and examples that can be drawn from it. And as preteens become teens, they need still more detailed information that helps further define the complexity of situations they may face and helps them make tough choices in potentially difficult and important situations. For all youngsters, having information well ahead of the time that they need to make choices is always preferable.

Teach by Example

Parents can provide powerful, non-verbal messages to their children by defining and expressing values through their own actions in everyday life. Parents who participate in their communities by volunteering serve as great role models for their children. Values such as compassion and generosity toward others are demonstrated through donating clothing or food to shelters, taking a meal to a sick neighbor, or expending effort toward humanitarian or environmental concerns.

In many families, values are conveyed through particular religious practices and beliefs. The fundamental concepts in all religions of goodness, spirituality, and morality are the backbone of the family unit. They form the blueprint by which family members cultivate good relationships and happy lives as they practice their religion together and carry its teachings out into their society.

Teach by Sharing Concepts

The importance of such concepts as honesty and trust in relationships in both personal life and in society cannot be overstated. Personal accountability promotes an inner sense of strength and autonomy. Parents who value honesty can convey this to their children by pointing out occasions in which truthfulness plays a vital part in the outcome of a decision. Needless to say, children will learn that they do not always get what they want even if they are honest; nevertheless, being honest is always a superior choice and feels better than the alternative. Parents can provide children opportunities to practice honesty as well as other value-related concepts.

Teach by "What if . . .?"

Youngsters enjoy the "what if . . .?" game as a way of role-playing in preparation for future possibilities, and many opportunities arise with youngsters of all ages. The "what if . . .?" game gives kids a trial run—a testing opportunity to think ahead about situations when particular values may be called into play. Look at "what if-ing" as a chance to further enhance your relationship with your child and to prepare him or her for decision making. Children love hearing about parents' vulnerabilities as they experience morally based struggles. So tell your kids stories about times in your life when you had to make difficult choices and found it hard sticking to your values.

Teach by Recognizing Values in Others

Parents can transmit values to their children indirectly by exposing their kids to others who actively exemplify these virtues. Good principles learned from religious beliefs, or practiced by a sports hero, teacher, friend, or by a character in a favorite book can be singled out by parents as useful examples of high morality. Hopefully, values that children learn while living at home are internalized and eventually are practiced easily and naturally.

Teach by Empowering Children

There is nothing as desirable to children as the acceptance, praise, and attention of their parents. Therefore, parents can seize opportunities to reward youngsters for displaying esteemed values in everyday life. As a result, children will beam with pride and repeat the lauded behavior. With each repetition, and the praise accompanying it, behavior is likely to become more natural—the value is thus instilled.

Take Advantage of the Media

Opportunities to review sexual values with children present themselves constantly. Most TV programs are inundated with sexual messages that provide occasions to discuss moral principles. It is impossible to monitor all or most of these messages; but it is worth parents' whole-hearted attempt. Our efforts toward well-intentioned censorship tells our kids how protective we are of our family's values. When we watch TV with them, we will see codes of conduct dramatized that do not reflect our own. These instances, of course, provide teachable moments for discussing and reiterating our beliefs. We can take these opportunities to talk about how we feel about drugs, alcohol, and sex, keeping in mind that our *actions* will speak louder than our words.

Just like other issues about sexuality, children's values are molded, not only by their families, but also by friends, religion, TV, school, and society as a whole. Therefore, it is through their thorough understanding of the essence of the virtues we stand by, that our children are most likely to embrace and live by these morals themselves and reject others that are less healthy for them.

27

THE ART OF COMMUNICATION

What does communication have to do with sexuality? Everything! When children learn how to communicate their needs, their concerns, and their feelings, they nurture their own sense of individuality and sexuality and they feel safe relating with other people. Communication gets us what we want; sometimes it keeps us from getting what we do not want.

When children are infants, they communicate with us through nonverbal messages to get their needs met. As children get older, they start to talk, conveying their desires more clearly. During their early school years, kids add reading and writing to their communication abilities. And when they become preteens, another aspect of communication should be practiced diligently. It is the art of *listening*.

Unfortunately, while the majority of adults have learned the basic skills of reading, writing, and speaking, far fewer demonstrate an ability to listen. This lack becomes a crucial flaw during our parenting years. If the parent's audio receiver is not operational, communication lines ultimately jam. If, however, we parents learn to listen to our children when they are young, maybe they will listen to us later! So, how do we bring ourselves up to speed?

Mirroring Listening

"Mirroring listening" is a technique that allows communication between two individuals. It simply means taking the time to listen carefully, without preconceived ideas or opinions, to what the other person is saying. It also requires that the person listening be willing not to offer solutions. As an empathic listener, the parent should try to restate the child's words, and/or label the underlying feeling the child may be experiencing. This is an attempt to clarify the child's statements and, at the same time, to acknowledge that the parent really has understood what the child meant to say. Of course, mirroring listening takes time, effort, and, most of all, practice.

Many times, when listening to their children, parents are too quick to respond by offering solutions, insights, and reprimands. This behavior can, at times, send the message to our children that they are not capable of handling their own problems. When our children react in self-protective ways by constructing mental walls, it can keep communication between us at bay. For example, Jocelyn comes home from school, visibly upset.

> Mom (trying to cheer her up): "How was your day?"
> Jocelyn: "It was terrible. Emily stole my pencil and she wouldn't give it back to me."
> Mom: "Well, did you tell the teacher?"
> Jocelyn: "No."
> Mom: "You need to tell the teacher, or, if you're not willing to do that, tell Emily to give back the pencil. It's not right for kids to take things that don't belong to them. It's against the rules. You know it's not right; why did you let her do that to you?"

Mom's part in the exchange is a lecture and an accusation all in one, and by the time this mother is done talking, Jocelyn has slumped into her seat, feeling defeated and trapped. On the other hand, if Mom had taken the time to listen and had not jumped to conclusions so quickly, another scenario might have evolved.

> Mom (trying to cheer her up): "How was your day?"
>
> Jocelyn: "It was terrible. Emily stole my pencil and she wouldn't give it back to me."
>
> Mom: "Oh dear!" (Pause.)
>
> Jocelyn: "Yeah, and I got so angry I nearly punched her. Then the teacher saw us and told us to 'figure it out.'"
>
> Mom: "You got angry at Emily, and Mrs. Weber tried to help?"
>
> Jocelyn: "You know, Emily did give me back my pencil, but she isn't my friend anymore."
>
> Mom: "Sounds like you're still angry at Emily for taking your pencil."
>
> Jocelyn: "It'll be OK tomorrow."

Mirroring Listening Dos

- Practice when there's plenty of time. The morning rush may not be an appropriate opportunity to mirror listen.
- Make eye contact to express warmth and openness.
- Rephrase or restate the content of your child's message as you heard it.
- Clarify any misinterpretations you may have made.
- Acknowledge your child's perspective.
- Use "I" statements when appropriate.
- Offer opinions only if asked.

Mirroring Listening Don'ts

- Don't interrupt.
- Avoid analyzing, suggesting, or moralizing.
- Avoid asking questions designed to get more information or just to appear interested.
- Do not minimize your child's concerns with humor or sarcasm.

Here are some phrases that help parents convey a willingness to listen without being judgmental:

- "You must have had a good reason to do that."
- "I only can imagine how confusing it must be for you."
- "I want to hear more about it."

Recognizing Feelings

One of the most valuable roles parents can play in their children's lives is that of teaching them to recognize their feelings. Being able to identify emotions is a learning process that begins as early as eighteen months of age. There are several major emotions human beings can experience, and we are healthier when we allow ourselves to own them all. Feelings are neither right nor wrong; they just *are*. Therefore, it is not wrong to be angry, sad, glad, unhappy, hateful, or loving in response to various situations. What *is* important is the way we act on feelings, because the way we express our emotions in words and actions affects our relationships with people and influences the way we see ourselves as well.

When children reach the age of two or three years, they are explosions of language skills and emotional growth, and learning to identify particular emotions is a process that involves time and patience. Parents can help children by identifying aloud the different emotions that they see them to express (e.g., "You got angry at Mary"). This labeling can be extremely helpful for children and eventually allows them to master (identify, accept, and deal with) the feelings.

In addition to listening to children, parents can demonstrate effective ways of communicating themselves. They should state their own feelings clearly using "I" statements: "I am angry when," or, "I like it when." Children will begin to assimilate these skills the more they are exposed to them. Learning new communication and listening skills takes practice, but is well worth the effort. Good communication helps children build self-esteem and enables them to understand others as well as themselves. Good communication is essential in all relationships, including marriage.

Being able to share personal feelings is a part of loving and being loved. In fact, some experts suggest that love is not possible between people who do not actively experience a full range of emotions. Therefore, it is healthy for children to practice expressing their feelings to those adults who care for them in a safe space with unconditional love. They can learn to identify what situations trigger a particular emotion and what they can do to resolve an uncomfortable feeling or retrieve a good one. "Swallowing" or "stuffing down" emotions never works, and, sooner or later, distances people from themselves and from significant others.

Nonverbal Communication

In addition to communicating through speaking and listening, nonverbal communication constitutes an enormous part of everyday exchange. When children (or adults) slam a door, scream, pout, hit, or ignore, a clear, unspoken message is conveyed that says, "I am not happy." Learning to read the underlying messages in these nonverbal encounters is one of the communication skills that children can begin to learn and understand. However, remember that nonverbal communication is usually less effective than verbal, and that clear, spoken messages reduce the danger of misinterpretation that often results from reading minds, sounds, or even faces.

Children who are able to communicate their feelings, needs, and concerns lay good foundations for interpersonal relationships. These skills are imperative for healthy sexual development. Through teaching youngsters the art of communication, parents grow along with their kids. Although initially difficult to master, with practice, both verbal and listening skills can enhance all relationships among people who use them.

28

▲▲▲

DECISION MAKING

M aking decisions is an integral part of life for adults and for children. Making good choices is monumentally important when the issues involve health and sexuality.

Children need opportunities to practice decision-making skills in situations that are appropriate for their developmental level. There are certainly problems that children can solve effectively if given the chance. As they practice making choices, they also learn that there are consequences associated with their decisions. Too often, parents feel that being a good parent means solving all of their children's problems for them. But a parent's role as sole problem-solver is not beneficial to children because it sends a clear message that youngsters are not capable of finding solutions to their own problems and, therefore, that they must rely on others. This practice ultimately establishes overdependent adults who may be less effective mates and parents themselves.

Children should practice their decision-making skills from an early age and during everyday situations. For example, a young preschooler can be offered at least two options about what to wear, what toy to play with, and who to have over. These and other similar age-appropriate opportunities for choice will help the child develop this basic talent. The more possibilities available to children, the more they will learn about the difficulties of choosing. Eventually, they will gain confidence in their ability to make good decisions by themselves, in all areas, including those that affect their sexuality.

At the same time, children must learn that all decisions have consequences, and by allowing children to experience the consequences, they learn valuable lessons. For example, Nathan, age twelve, wants a buzz haircut and pleads with his parents to take him to the local barber. His mother notes potential good and bad points. Buzz cuts are easy to take care of and are very "in," but Nathan may not like the new look on him. Nevertheless, the final decision is left to Nathan. Alas! He hates his new haircut. His friends tease him because he looks weird. Mom is supportive of his choice and does not insult him for his decision. Instead, she reassures him that some choices do not meet our expectations; and luckily, the hair will grow back quickly. In this case, Nathan learns an important lesson about consequences. Youngsters will be confronted with sexual decisions many times during their preteen and teen years. Some of their choices may involve sexual activity versus abstinence. Other decisions will concern relationships, sexual health, and drugs. Each choice will bear a consequence.

It is crucial for children to witness their parents solving problems and making joint decisions during daily family life. Parents should involve children in the process of selecting family activities and outings, and in other areas in which choices will influence the entire family. However, there are many decisions children are not capable of making and that rightly belong to parents. Deciding which choices belong to the child and which to the parent is sometimes difficult. Children mature at different rates, and some are more adept at logical reasoning than others. Each family must decide in which situations and at what age a child should be allowed to make final decisions. Many issues are obvious, such as those dealing with safety. Children should *not* have a choice about whether to buckle-up in their car seats, to use protective safety gear while playing sports, or to be immunized. Other decisions are more ambiguous. For example:

At what age might a girl start shaving her legs?
What and how much should a child eat?
How late can the preteen stay up at night?
How much effort should be put into schoolwork?

As children get older, they are able to handle more responsibility and can make choices about more complex matters. A goal of parenting is to relinquish power to children gradually as they grow, allowing them to take more responsibility for their actions and to experience the consequences of their decisions. The fact is that by the time children start making sexual decisions, they are no longer under the direct influence of their parents; so, the more practice they get deciding everyday issues for themselves, the more capable they will be to make good choices about more challenging sexual issues later on. Whenever it is possible and realistic, parents should inspire their children's confidence to make choices and should support them, even if they would have decided differently from their youngster. This empowers children by providing them with a sense of being equal, autonomous members of the family. This, in turn, contributes greatly to their sense of self-worth.

If the outcome of children's decisions are good, their egos grow a bit; if they are not, natural consequences will teach valuable lessons, and similar mistakes may be avoided in the future. Whatever parents' personal limitations on their children's decision making, youngsters *should* be allowed to make choices related to personal taste. The color and combination of clothing, the style (within reason), and haircuts are examples of such decisions. Respect children's individuality.

These are some key points to keep in mind when thinking about children's decision-making skills.

- Give your children the opportunity to make decisions by offering them age-appropriate choices—the younger the child, the fewer the number of choices; the older the child, the more. Here are some examples of choices that children, based on their ages, can practice making:
  — What clothes to wear. If they choose the wrong clothing for the weather, they will learn what it feels like to be too cold or too hot.
  — Whether or not to eat. If Andrew chooses not to eat lunch, for example, he will be hungry by mid-afternoon. To experience hunger is a powerful motivator.
  — Whether or not to use the toilet. This bodily function should be left entirely up to your school-age child.
- Provide your young child with alternatives that are acceptable to both of you. If you offer two choices, make sure you can live with either.
- Step back and allow the outcome to unfold once a decision is made. Natural consequences are powerful teachers.
- Never say, "I told you so!" when dealing with a child's negative consequence.
- Praise the outcome of good choices, especially those related to issues of health. Say:
  — "You're eating such healthy foods."
  — "You are really taking good care of yourself."
  — "You make good choices."
  — "You have great ideas!"

- Set an example for your child through your own wise choices about lifestyle, values, relationships, and parenting techniques.
- Talk to your children about the process of analyzing and taking time to make the right decision, especially when difficult choices arise.
- Review your values with your youngster. Being sexual or not with another individual is a choice.
- Make sure your youngsters know you are available to help them when difficult decisions do arise.

Learning how to make good decisions takes practice. It is never too early to start, and this skill is never too polished. Children who practice making good choices will have a head start toward becoming responsible, healthy adults capable of making well-informed decisions about life's bigger quandaries, including choices of sexual behavior.

29

‸‸

PROBLEM SOLVING

The social skills necessary for dealing effectively with problems are useful on a daily basis. In any personal relationship, conflicts are inevitable; yet, there are practical ways of dealing with personal differences. Children who learn to solve problems effectively can make and enforce healthy choices about their own sexuality and are more likely to become happy, responsible, assertive adults. Parents can teach their children to be assertive in ways that convey respect; to negotiate in situations where answers are not agreed upon; and to seek help from others when solutions seem evasive. With practice, your children can become experts in problem solving.

Assertiveness

The old adage, "Children should be seen and not heard," has finally withered and died. Often parents who grew up in families where silence prevailed at the dinner table feel awkward with, and challenged by, their children's assertiveness. But psychologists believe that children have a right and a responsibility to express themselves and must learn how to do so while respecting the rights of others. Through this assertiveness, they can grow into adults who take responsibility for themselves, their actions, and the consequences of those actions.

As children become preteens, speaking up and expressing needs becomes even more crucial. One of the most important areas where assertiveness training pays off is in dealing with issues about sexuality. Sexual molestation, date rape, abstinence, and setting limits on relationships are all issues about which kids must speak up. The more practice they get as young children, the better they will do when they face more challenging situations that require value-related stands.

Assertiveness must be balanced with respect. The line is often fine between respectful solicitation and rudeness. Every exchange between an adult and child or a child and a peer should be polite. Common obstacles to effective assertiveness training occurs in youngsters who are shy and/or oversensitive. Bashful children feel their needs but do not express them. So children who are shy, introverted, or particularly sensitive need more encouragement and support as they learn and practice putting themselves forward.

One way of helping preteens overcome their fear of assertiveness, is to role-play potential situations they may encounter. A parent can be the youngster in the scenario and the youngster, the adult, or vice versa. For example, Andrew wants to ride on the fourth grade field trip in the same car as Brian, but he has been assigned to Anna's mother's car. Andrew is mortified since he wants to be with Brian so the others won't tease him about riding with Anna. Andrew's mother decides to role-play a conversation between Andrew and his teacher, Mrs. Crawford. Andrew will play himself and his mother will play Mrs. Crawford.

Andrew: "Mrs. Crawford, I really would like to ride in the same car as Brian."

Mom (posing as Mrs. Crawford): "I'm sorry, Andrew, but I have already assigned you to Anna's car."

Andrew, addressing his mother: "See. Mrs. Crawford won't change her mind just because I ask her to."

Mom: "Hang on Andrew. You need to tell her why it bothers you."

Andrew: "O.K., I'll try again. Mrs. Crawford, I would like to ride with Brian because he is my friend. It is a long trip and I don't like it when kids tease me about being with Anna."

Mom (as Mrs. Crawford): "Well, Andrew, how about Anna's feelings?"

Andrew: "What if I explain to Anna that it's not anything against her. It's just that Brian and I are good friends."

Mom (as Mrs. Crawford): "O.K., Andrew. If you and Anna can work it out, it's fine with me."

Andrew to his mother: "But Mom, she isn't going to say that!"

Mom: "She may not, but at least you will have expressed yourself and can feel good about talking with your teacher about your feelings. Try it out and see."

Role-playing can address many situations other than school quandaries. Youngsters can also have pretend phone conversations with friends of the opposite sex, coaches, or siblings.

Compromising and Negotiating

Resolving problems through compromise is negotiation, and we all do it. When parents of young children say, "Let's clean up your room; then we'll go and play," it is a way of teaching children the art of compromise while still getting their needs met. The message is understood: "If we clean this room first, we get to play. If we don't, we won't." Any minor problem can be presented as a negotiable issue and, as such, it provides useful practice. Such problem solving can be fun, rewarding, and interesting.

Children should understand that the first step in negotiation is to identify their needs and state them clearly. Obviously there will be situations in which youngsters will not get what they want, but they should be assured that nothing can happen if they do not ask. The next step is finding a compromise that makes the goal realizable. Be sure your child understands

131

that it is important not to give up values and beliefs in an effort to come to terms. This is, of course, very important when sexual issues are concerned. Reassure your youngster that when a negotiation is not headed in the right direction and goals seem unattainable, compromise can be found and conflicts may be solved with the help of others, such as family members, teachers, or professionals.

Seeking Help

Luckily most problems are everyday glitches with simple solutions. However, as the complexity of a problem increases, children should be certain that parents and family members are there to help them cope. They must be assured that asking for help is a smart way to solve a problem. Finally, youngsters should understand that aid comes in many forms. A listening ear, a phone call or note at the right moment, or any kind gesture all qualify. Many public schools have introduced the popular "Conflict Resolution Program" to teach same-aged peers how to handle conflict amongst themselves.

Parents decide for young children when problems require professional aid. But, as youngsters get older, they should be aware that professional help is available and desirable when a problem feels too big to solve alone or with parents. Parents can tell their children about instances when they availed themselves of outside assistance to solve a problem or deal with a big change. Situations such as buying a new home, planning a vacation, learning to play an instrument, treating medical problems, or facing difficult financial circumstances are those in which professionals can help. Parents certainly must step in immediately and find help for their children when they are hurt, depressed, into alcohol or drugs, or are generally in peril.

Key Points about Problem Solving for Parents
• All children have a right to express their needs and feelings to parents or other trusted adults.

- Being able to express one's needs while respecting the needs of others is an essential skill. This is the difference between assertiveness and aggressiveness.
- Youngsters have the right to say how they feel even if they do not agree with others.
- Honesty is essential when communicating one's needs.
- Practice negotiating with children about everyday issues such as chores, TV viewing, allowance, and so on.
- Use examples from everyday life when, as an adult, you have needed to seek help in order to solve a problem.
- Be sensitive about adult conflicts that do not concern children. Marital difficulties, financial woes, or trouble with in-laws should not be discussed in front of children.
- Kids who problem solve well can enforce healthy choices about their own sexuality and are more likely to become happy, responsible assertive adults.

Problem solving, a skill called into play throughout life, constantly merits review and practice. As children grow, their needs change and they, too, need to learn and participate in increasingly complicated problem-solving solutions. In personal relationships, outcomes of debates over sensitive, sometimes sexual, issues can solidify or shake delicate balances. Therefore, particular care should be exercised to allot the necessary time, patience and fair techniques to sensitive problems. Ultimately, children will use these learned talents outside their families in dealing with peers, teachers, and future mates.

30

SEXUAL CURIOSITY

As children begin to explore the world beyond their own boundaries, they experience a natural curiosity about same- and opposite-sex private body parts. Girls are interested in what boys' genitals look like and vice versa. This is particularly so if a child does not have a sibling of the opposite sex or has not had an opportunity during the course of family life to catch a glimpse of a member of the opposite sex in the nude. For most parents, this stage of normal, sexual curiosity is the first real instance when they are faced with having to set boundaries around socially acceptable sexual behavior.

Children will take the opportunity during typical play to get physically close to same- or opposite-sex children to discover what they look like. The most common scenario is enacted when kids play doctor. Most children experience visits to their physician or healthcare provider during which their bodies are examined, so they choose to dramatize this event during play in order to catch a peak at another body.

Parents should be aware that children play sexual games out of curiosity, and this is normal. When parents discover their child naked, or partially dressed, in the presence of another child, their reaction is crucial to the child's future sense of his or her own body and its privacy. Parents need not panic, scold, or punish. However, they *do* need to set guidelines for future, appropriate, sexual conduct.

Sensitive Handling of Sexual Limits
SCENARIO # 1

Your five-year-old son has a playmate in your home and you notice they are particularly quiet. You go to see what they are up to and walk in on them. There they are—naked from the waist down. How do you respond?

A situation like this feels stressful to most parents, but prior preparation can allow adults at least to appear calm. Do not shout or reprimand the youngsters, but, instead, set guidelines for children in your home. You may say something like, "I want you both to put your clothes back on. Your bodies are private, and we do not take our clothes off at other people's homes. Let's find something else for you two to do."

Whether or not to share the incident with the other child's parent is a personal decision, but, as a general rule, reporting what transpired at your home to the friend's parent is advisable. This occasion can be turned into a teachable moment for both children within their respective families. Without overwhelming your child, you can describe acceptable sexual limits. This next step prevents mixed feelings of guilt or distrust on the part of the child. If the children continue to play doctor, this may indicate that their curiosity is still unsatisfied. Sit down with your own child and review the basic information about what naked bodies look like, naming the different body parts as you go. At this age, most children will be satisfied. If your child still has questions, don't hesitate to respond. Avoid postponing queries. Hopefully, the other child's parents will do the same!

When should you be concerned?

- If the nude interaction occurs between children whose ages differ by four or five years or more. This creates a situation in which an older child may abuse his power over a younger child.
- If the situation appears to have been forced upon a child against her will.
- If your child seems withdrawn, excessively teary, or his or her behavior changes dramatically after the interlude. In this case, professional help may be required to sort through the feelings you and your child are experiencing.

What if your child refuses to listen or seems uncommunicative about a sexual incident?

Your child's temperament may be very sensitive. Silence and a refusal to discuss the situation may ensue. It is not uncommon for children to feel embarrassed when they talk about their bodies and sex, especially if they sense that they have done something wrong. In addition, they may not know how to verbalize their confusion or how to sort out the meaning of what has happened. Although fragile feelings should be respected, a parent's role must be to provide children with pertinent information whether they seem to be paying attention or not. If they refuse to listen, or simply walk away, tell them that you have a book that you will leave for them to look at if they want to. Some older youngsters are more comfortable with this approach, especially when the parent is trying to teach them about the opposite sex. Allow your child some time and the privacy necessary to process the information. After a couple of days, ask matter-of-factly if the information you gave them was looked at and if there are any questions.

SCENARIO # 2
A toddler is taking a bath and starts touching his or her genitals.

This is a very common scenario that repeats itself several times in most households. When this happens, take the opportunity to review the names of the different body parts with your child. Try a matter-of-fact approach. Begin by naming a nonsexual body part; then scatter in the sexual ones with the rest. Use correct names from the very beginning. (For a review of the correct anatomical terms, see Key 8). At the same time, tell your child that bodies are private. Be explicit when describing what you mean by *private* (see Key 2). *Private body parts* refers to the areas of their bodies covered by bathing suits. For boys, this includes the penis, testicles, and buttocks; for girls, it means breasts, vulvas, and buttocks. Children should understand that no one should touch their private body parts, nor should they show those parts to anyone. Of course, exceptions occur when a parent helps bathe children or when a physician conducts check-ups or treats for illness or injury.

Modesty at Home

Setting guidelines and boundaries about nudity and communal showers may be evidence of the first real acceptance by many parents that their children are truly separate sexual beings. It is not uncommon for a busy mother, when trying to get herself and the rest of the family ready, to jump into the shower with a toddler or two in tow. It is quick, efficient, and it gets the job done. So, at what point do parents deserve privacy in the shower; or, even more important, at what point do our children deserve privacy in the bathroom? Like many aspects of parenting, there is no right age at which a parent absolutely should not shower with their children, but there are clear guidelines that may help families with this decision.

Children are sexual beings just like we adults although they do not have the capacity yet to understand the complexity of sexual issues or to express intense sexual feelings. Nevertheless, seeing the opposite or same sex naked may excite and confuse children.

The first sign a parent receives while showering with an opposite-sex child that indicates they both need privacy is when the child stares at the parent's nude body to the point where the adult feels uncomfortable. A little modesty is now in order. By covering our bodies in front of our children, we teach them how to behave and, at the same time, indicate the degree of privacy we are comfortable with. Covering up denotes a sense of respect for the body.

Usually, by the time most youngsters have reached age seven or eight, parents notice their reluctance to shower with an adult or to be seen naked. Most nine- and ten-year-olds are mortified if a parent walks in on them while they shower. Prepubertal youngsters should be respected and provided with bathroom privacy. By noticing a child's clues, parents can respond appropriately to their child's need for privacy just as the child learns from the parent.

31

~~~~~~

ABSTINENCE

Abstinence, defined as not engaging in any form of sexual activity that could lead to pregnancy or sexually transmitted infections, is a surprisingly stress-free topic to discuss with preteens since most children this age cannot imagine why anyone would ever want to "do it" anyhow! (Parents can reassure their children that they probably will feel differently as they get older.) Waiting to engage in sexual intercourse until a young person is really ready, whether that point is reached in young adulthood, in a committed relationship, or in marriage, is by far the healthiest and safest way to enjoy this aspect of sexuality. "Really ready" means being fully informed and having fully considered decisions and their consequences. As children become teenagers and young adults, they are able to understand that practicing abstinence can allow for alternatives to or postponement of intercourse if that is their choice.

Regardless of our parental opinions and rules, children have the final vote as to whether they will abstain from sexual activity or not. This means that if we parents hope to affect this important choice, we must start early. We should define our own codes of behavior, practice them, and teach them to our children. If children are used to making decisions based upon the morals they grow up with, they will be more likely to stick to their principles in sexual situations later on.

In addition, sexual decisions are easier for teens and young adults if they regularly utilize the interpersonal skills of communication and assertiveness that help in the decision-making process. Parents should help children cultivate these necessary skills so they can make decisions that will keep them sexually healthy and responsible in the future. If children grow up in environments where they are listened to and respected as individuals, they are more likely to expect this behavior in future relationships. Enhancing children's self-esteem in as many ways as you can will help give your youngsters the inner strength to stick to their values and choose abstinence if they believe this is the right decision for them. Allow and encourage them to grow as individuals, and teach them it is O.K. to be different from their peers.

The more information children have ahead of time, the more apt they are to choose wisely in a difficult situation. If parents want their youngster to choose abstinence, they should offer them guidance about self-control, about how to avoid potentially awkward or dangerous situations, how to consider alternatives to intercourse, and how to seek help if it's needed. Provide the stability of a family home where answers to their questions are readily available. If this is not feasible because of your parenting style, provide other resources. Books, mentors, family members, and community and religious groups can provide direction as long as their values are in harmony with yours.

Parents should know that many youngsters confuse or equate sexual intercourse with being grown up. Sometimes they try to prove their maturity by engaging in sexual relationships before they acquire the emotional adult status that prepares them for intercourse. Therefore, in addition to the physical deterrents to early sex (pregnancy, parenthood, STDs) parents should emphasize the severe emotional consequences that can result. You can convey to your children that, indeed the sexual drive is intense as hormones rage in young bodies. But, before giving in to their physical urges through a sexual commitment, young people should make an equally intense emotional one. This will require time to develop friendship based upon shared communication, values, and goals. Without mutual emotional commitment and understanding between potential sexual partners, the possibility of grief for one or both is high.

While open communication between parents and their children is the most desired approach to resolving sexual issues, we know that, in reality, as youngsters enter their teen years, they may not be willing to share any aspects of their sexual life with their parents. This is part of a normal separation process that commences as youngsters get older; their need for privacy should be respected. If face-to-face talks are not feasible at this age, parents should offer to share information with them about abstinence and how to maintain that position if that is their choice. Once again, books, respected adults, or health care providers can provide support.

Key Points about Addressing Abstinence with Preteens

- Abstinence means not engaging in sexual activity that will lead to pregnancy or STDs.
- Children and preteens are not ready for sexual intercourse.
- Although many teens are sexually active, they are usually not emotionally mature enough to be sexually involved.
- Youngsters will be healthier and happier if they postpone sexual intercourse until they are young adults.
- A family's value system plays a vital role in a youngster's self-esteem and in his or her ability to make good choices about sexuality.

Abstinence is a very sensitive issue for many families. An individual's decision whether or not to be abstinent is based upon family and religious values, self-esteem, communication skills, and the degree of emotional maturity. All of these factors are developed and conveyed through diverse life experiences.

141

32

~~~~~~

MASTURBATION AND SELF-PLEASURING

M asturbation is playing with, touching, or rubbing your own sex organs for pleasure. The *topic* is one many adults are uncomfortable discussing. The *practice* is even less acceptable to others, especially if they suspect their own children are masturbating. Often these strong feelings are rooted in religious beliefs. But regardless of the source of the sometimes negative value judgments about masturbation, it *is* a subject filled with controversy, taboos, and differing ideas about what is and is not acceptable. The intent of this chapter is neither to present a historical interpretation of its origin, nor to pass judgment on individual opinions about masturbation, but to present the facts and allow parents to decide how to approach this subject with their own children.

Male fetuses have been documented having erections while in the mother's womb. Penile erections can be noted during diaper changes. Initially, as babies discover their bodies, they may finger their genitals in the same way they do ears or elbows. With repeated manipulation, they discover the pleasurable sensation resulting from touching themselves. Most three-year-olds overtly touch their genitals as they start to explore the world and themselves within it. Boys who are potty trained experience more pleasurable feelings as their penises are freed from the constraints of diapers, and additional rubbing can occur. It is no wonder that many three-year-old boys always have their hands in their pants as they discover this fascinating part of their body. At this age, children may masturbate quite freely several times a day, or they may not do it at all.

Girls' genitals are more concealed and not as prominent as boys' are. Nevertheless, little girls do discover their clitoris and the pleasurable feeling that rubbing causes. An occasional young girl may stroke her nipples as a way of soothing herself to sleep. Most commonly, children touch their genitals playfully during bath time, when they are tired, bored, reading, or during long car trips. If you discover your child masturbating, the attitude you project at that moment can determine the youngster's long-term impressions of his or her body.

Our role as parents should be one of guidance, not condemnation. We need to explain to children that it is not appropriate to masturbate publicly while, at the same time, conveying the message that their bodies are good, pleasurable, and private. We parents should be prepared before the need arises to tell our children what we want them to know about masturbation.

As youngsters enter their teen and young adulthood years, they begin to experiment with other aspects of sexual pleasure such as kissing, hugging, and touching one another. These ways of sharing sexual pleasure with others are integral parts of healthy sexuality. Other sensitive topics that may arise during the teen years include discussing alternatives to intercourse as ways to prevent pregnancy and sexually transmitted infections. Obviously, children under the age of twelve or thirteen are not developmentally ready for the details of these topics of sexuality, yet as parents, we need to learn or remind ourselves that being sexual with another person involves more than sexual intercourse.

Key Points about Masturbation that Parents Should Consider

- Masturbation is one way individuals express their sexuality.
- The facts are clear: Masturbation does not cause any physical or mental harm to a person's body.
- If you discover your child masturbating, do not panic. Remember, this is a very normal way for children to discover and explore the parts of their bodies.
- If you walk into your child's bedroom during quiet time while he or she is masturbating, excuse yourself and allow them privacy.
- If your child is masturbating in a socially inappropriate setting, intervene by saying something like, "I know it feels good to touch your body like that, but this is not an acceptable place. In the future, I would like you to go to the bathroom or to the privacy of your bedroom."
- If you feel your child is spending so much time masturbating that its practice is interfering with the enjoyment of other childhood activities, it is time to seek professional help. Speak to your child's physician.
- Parents need to have a clear idea of their beliefs about masturbation.
- Encourage your child to speak to you about sexuality. If this is not comfortable for you, find a suitable trusted adult who can help.

33

~~~~~~

WELLNESS AND DISEASE PREVENTION

M ost parents agree that, above all, health is the top priority for themselves and for family members. Wellness is a condition of a child's life that we and they take for granted. With the exception of recurrent colds that children suffer during their years in daycare and preschool, they are generally quite healthy. Nevertheless, we should teach children that caring for one's body is a lifelong responsibility. Personal hygiene should begin during the toddler years when our children first learn to use the toilet and wash their hands. It continues into adult life when maturing girls learn how to care for themselves during menstruation and when both males and females take precautions to prevent venereal disease and to protect emotional well-being through healthy sexual decisions. Illnesses, such as cancer, although not contagious or well-understood, possibly may be prevented or slowed through incorporating healthy habits into our daily lives that will promote wellness and longevity.

Wellness and the Preschooler

As children grow and begin to comprehend the concept of hygiene, they can understand that germs are responsible for the transmission of disease. Since germs live in body fluids such as saliva, sharing toothbrushes and eating utensils can spread germs and cause illness. Children can also understand that the body uses much of the food that they provide it; the portion not required is eliminated through urination and bowel movements. These are essential, normal bodily functions.

Taking care of one's body includes keeping all parts of it clean. As soon as preschoolers are potty trained, they should be taught to wipe properly, from front to back. Parents can say, "When you urinate, wipe your vulva from front to back. If you have a bowel movement, take another piece of toilet paper and wipe your buttocks from front to back, too." Wiping this way prevents germs that normally reside in the feces from spreading from the anus to the vulva area. Boys do not have this problem. Like all healthy habits, proper hygiene takes practice, and children need reminders and constant praise for trying as they learn.

Another basic health measure that cannot be emphasized enough is hand washing. The simple measure of using soap and water after going to the bathroom, before preparing or eating meals, and during acute illnesses such as upper respiratory colds, helps reduce the spread of germs.

Young children can also learn to take precautions when it comes to injuries that cause bleeding. They should be advised not to touch another person's blood because blood can contain germs that could make them sick. Instead, they should call a teacher, parent, or other trusted adult right away.

Wellness and the Preteen

As parents, we can help ensure our children's healthy sexual lives by promoting pride in their good general health and hygiene. During the preteen years, children will naturally show interest in their bodies and how they function. From ages eight to twelve, most youngsters may still need occasional reminders about brushing their teeth, taking daily showers, and using deodorant. Routine visits by all family members to dentists and health care providers underscore the importance of ongoing health vigilance. In addition, healthy, adult habits are established as youngsters gradually learn to assume responsibility for getting adequate sleep and exercise.

Major threats to your preteen's health are accidents, like car crashes, sports injuries, and falls. Kids this age often seem reckless. Remind them frequently that they must be careful when they play, and correct them when you see them engaged in dangerous activities. Protective sports gear and seat belts are mandatory even though children will fight you on the former issue. Kids often accuse their parents of overprotectiveness; but they love knowing you care.

Parents can be models for children's behavior by showing them the importance of taking care of one's body and by promoting basic health habits, such as:

- Eating the right food. Provide your child with a variety of healthy, nutritious choices. The key is offering a balanced diet in which small amounts of the different food groups are available on a regular basis.
- Providing opportunities for regular exercise as a way to invigorate the body and maintain cardiovascular health. Exercise is an opportunity to share wonderful family time.
- Washing hands regularly can eliminate many germs that cause common cold symptoms. Wash hands before meals, after using the bathroom, and after outside play.
- Encouraging children to talk to you when something about their body worries them.
- Visiting your health care provider and dentist on a regular basis to set good examples about the importance of preventive health measures.
- Encouraging children's good health habits through education, example, praise and encouragement.

Our goal as parents is to teach our children that good health depends, to a large degree, on choices over which they have control. From a very young age, children can assume responsibility for their own eating, sleeping, and bathroom habits. As they continue to grow, they should add to their responsibilities. Menstrual care, breast and testicular self-examinations, and the prevention of sexually transmitted disease help ensure good physical health and promote positive choices as youngsters experience their own sexuality. We owe it to our children to help them help themselves grow into healthy, responsible adults.

34

∧∧

CONTRACEPTION AND ABORTION

Today parents must address multiple difficult issues about their children's sexuality, including contraception and abortion. The age at which you broach these topics with your youngster varies according to your child's development and mental readiness, and depends upon your level of comfort and preparedness as well. For many parents, religious beliefs, moral ethics, and even politics affect their views about preventing or ending pregnancies. Parents must define their beliefs for themselves and then be willing to present and underscore them with their children as they share pertinent information about contraception and abortion.

Contraception

Contraception may be brought up quite easily during talks about puberty with preteens from ages eight to twelve. The task is pleasantly simple at this stage because, for these youngsters, the thought that parents may engage in sexual intercourse for any other reason than for making babies is shocking, disgusting, and completely implausible as one mother relates in the following story:

> "My son, age nine, once found a sealed condom in our bathroom. After he had opened it and discarded it, I found it and questioned him. He was curious about it, he admitted. I explained that it was to use during sexual intercourse to prevent us from having babies. My son was quite alarmed and said, 'But I thought you guys told me

you weren't having any more babies.' After I explained that he was absolutely right, but that we have sexual intercourse also to show affection and love, he blurted out, 'You mean you and Dad still do it?' It was hard to keep a straight face.

As his amazement illustrates, this child really just needs to know why, if his parents are "doing it" more often than he thinks, a baby does not result every time.

The following are simple explanations that may be used when addressing the topic of contraception with your child.

- Contraception means preventing pregnancy when having sexual intercourse.
- When adults have sexual intercourse, they may not want to have a baby, so they do different things to prevent a pregnancy from occurring. This is called contraception or birth control.
- There are many different types of contraception. (Parents may want to include a discussion of the method(s) of contraception that they feel most comfortable with, whether it is the rhythm method, condoms, the pill, and so forth. Lengthy explanations at this age are not necessary.)

Parents should keep in mind that their sexual life is private, and boundaries that guard that privacy need to be set and respected. It is not appropriate for parents to share the details of their personal sexual life with children. Answering a youngster's questions honestly can be accomplished without relinquishing the parent's own sense of personal privacy.

Abortion

It is unlikely that the topics of contraception or abortion will come up before youngsters start school, but parents should be prepared with simple, clear explanations in case they do. Older preteens, ages ten to twelve years, invariably will hear these terms on TV or at school. So if the subjects of abortion and contraception are not addressed at home, children will believe what they want about preventing or ending pregnancies, independent of your views. In this scenario, your family values are sacrificed to others. Talking about these issues does not suggest for a moment that parents condone one or both. It simply means you want to convey accurate information about contraception and abortion and, at the same time, define how you look at these issues within your value system. The following are some simple statements parents might use with preteen children when defining abortion.

- "Sometimes a woman who is pregnant decides not to have the baby, and the pregnancy is ended. She has an abortion."
- "Abortions are done in clinics, doctor's offices or some hospitals. They are performed by a physician or other health care provider."
- "If a woman who is pregnant decides she does not want to have an abortion, but is not ready to be a parent, she can place the baby for adoption when it is born."
- "Abortion is safe and legal in this country."

Parents should also discuss their own beliefs and values with their children about the topic of abortion.

Contraception and abortion are very controversial and emotional topics for many adults. Parents should reassure their children that, as they get older, they will develop their own opinions and values about these issues, just as they will about all others. Also, as they grow, kids will be able to assimilate more detailed information that will help them make sexual decisions more responsibly. At the same time, parents should remind children that sexual intercourse is an adult behavior. Time, maturity, and a commitment to oneself and the other person in the relationship are required to produce an adult, loving relationship.

35

~~~~~~

HIV/AIDS AND STDs

T alking to your children about HIV/AIDS can be as intimidating as talking to them about the facts of life. Unfortunately, children hear about HIV/AIDS from a variety of sources including TV, school, and adult conversation. From a child's point of view, the information about HIV/AIDS is sketchy, confusing, and frightening. What they know for sure is that it is a serious condition. They may be afraid to ask you about it depending upon the nature of the information they have heard outside the family. If they do ask, be prepared to answer. You will not need to have volumes of information at your fingertips. (It would be impossible for parents to keep up with all the latest developments about HIV.) Luckily, a child needs relatively simple information about the subject, so this quick course should help you.

HIV stands for *human immunodeficiency virus*. This virus is responsible for AIDS, or *acquired immune deficiency syndrome,* the latter stage of the HIV disease that is ultimately fatal. People who are infected with HIV can have the virus and not appear ill. It can take a long time, up to ten years, between the time that the virus is detected in a person's body and the appearance of disease. A very small proportion of people seem to resist the infection completely. The virus attacks the body's ability to fight infection. Thus, germs normally kept in check by the body's defenses, start to grow freely. These germs invade vital organs such as the lungs, liver, and brain, causing damage that leads to a breakdown in the body's ability to function and survive.

HIV can be acquired in any of the following ways:

- By being exposed to an infected person's body fluids, such as semen, vaginal secretions, blood, human breast milk, or any body fluid containing blood.
- By using needles for intravenous drug injections that have been used previously by people infected with the virus.
- By being born to a mother who has HIV.
- By using blood bank products. (Though this poses a very small risk of acquiring HIV.)
- By having unprotected sex with an infected individual.

At this time there is no cure or vaccine for HIV and AIDS. Although multiple research centers are collaborating to find a cure and halt the epidemic, the only effective strategy is prevention. New medications are tested regularly and diverse educational programs focus on teaching high-risk populations how to avoid contracting and spreading HIV.

Parents' role is to provide youngsters with age-appropriate information as questions or opportunities arise. Parents should not discuss explicit sexual behavior as they convey information about HIV/AIDS to children five through nine years of age; parents of children of any age can add to or delete any information offered here that does not conform to your moral values and standards. You are your child's main educator. So filter and add what is comfortable for you.

Answering Difficult Questions

The following is a sample conversation about HIV/AIDS. Parents may want to add to or modify it according to their child's developmental level.

> Child: "What is HIV?"
> Parent: "You have heard of HIV? At school, or where?"

Always inquire, without sounding accusatory or shocked, where and how the subject came up. Watch your body language; raised eyebrows are alarming. Then proceed.

> Parent: "HIV stands for human immunodeficiency virus. It is a germ that causes a serious illness. Remember last year when Jamie had chicken pox? Chicken pox is caused by a different kind of germ."

Use your child's demeanor to guide the conversation. Has your youngster left the room to play? If he or she is still sitting next to you, more can follow.

> Child: "Can *we* catch HIV?"
> Parent: "Well, HIV is spread from one person to another during sexual intercourse. Having sex with a person who has the HIV germ in his or her body can infect people. Also, using needles that have been used before by someone who has the HIV germ can give us the infection, so the doctor always uses new needles to give us shots. If a mother has the HIV germ in her body, her newborn baby could be born with the virus. I did not have the germ when you were born, and I do not have it now. You were born without it. Luckily, we don't have to worry about getting sick from HIV since we don't have the germ in our bodies."
> Child: "What is AIDS?"
> Parent: "Where did you hear about AIDS?"
> Child: "It was on TV. Someone was dying. Are we going to get it?"
> Parent: "No, we are not going to get AIDS. Luckily AIDS is very difficult to catch. You can't catch it like you do a cold or chicken pox."

This may be all that is needed for the younger child, say, from age five to seven. The older child, eight through twelve, may want more information and need further explanation.

> Parent: "AIDS stands for *acquired immunodeficiency syndrome.* It is a fancy name that doctors use to

refer to a person who has HIV and then gets very sick. HIV is the name of the germ that causes AIDS."

Child: "How do you get AIDS?"

Parent: "People who have AIDS have caught the HIV virus by having sex with someone who already had the virus (or germ). It also can happen through sharing needles for intravenous drugs, or being born to a mother who has the virus in her body."

Child: "Why do people who know they're sick have sex and babies when they know they could make other people sick?"

Parent: "Most of the time, people with the AIDS germ do not look or feel sick. They may not even know that they have HIV, so they may not take precautions to avoid passing the virus on to someone else."

Child: "What is a virus?"

Parent: "Remember, we've talked about germs— about washing our hands regularly and covering our noses and mouths when we sneeze. A virus is a germ that can make our bodies sick. Viruses cause chicken pox, the colds we get, and the stomach flu. Most times, our bodies fight off these viruses, and we get better in a few days. The HIV germ attacks our body's ability to fight off other germs. People with the HIV virus have a difficult time getting well when they are ill. Their bodies don't work as well."

Reassure your child that they cannot become infected with the HIV virus by hugging, touching, or being around someone who has the virus or AIDS. Once again, your child's attentiveness during your conversation can lead you further if necessary. If the conversation seems to have passed the fruitful point, take a breather and ask your child to explain all he or she now knows about HIV/AIDS. Always leave the door open for more discussions later; encourage your child to come back to you anytime with questions or concerns.

Sexually Transmitted Diseases

While you are discussing HIV/AIDS, you should acknowledge that there are several other sexually transmitted diseases. (Emphasize that intercourse is an adult behavior.) They include gonorrhea, syphilis, chlamydia, genital warts, and herpes. Although children need to know that part of adult life is taking responsibility for the health of one's body, it is not necessary to overwhelm them with all the potential illnesses that lurk in the world and their ugly manifestations. Sexuality is a beautiful part of adult life, but, like most other aspects of living, there are consequences to our actions. Children should understand that the risk of sexually transmitted diseases should be looked at like other adult actions with associated health risks.

As your children enter their teens, you should make them aware of additional information available to them about HIV and STDs. Other sources are health classes at school, physicians' offices, the local Planned Parenthood clinic, and libraries. (See Additional Resources.)

Key Points for Parents about Discussing HIV/AIDS and STDs

- More than anything, children want a responsive parent/adult to be willing to listen to them and answer their queries. Most of their questions will reflect an underlying concern about how HIV/AIDS might affect them or those close to them, for example, their parents.
- Your body language, facial expression, and overall demeanor will convey much more about your attitudes and values than your actual words will.
- You should determine where your child heard about HIV/AIDS or STDs. How did the subject come up? (Did he overhear it at school? On TV?)
- You should correct any misconceptions your child may have or correct any misinformation that you might have given her previously.

- You do not need to know all the answers right away. If your child asks you a difficult question and you are unsure of the answer, let your youngster know that you will find out and get back to him with the information. Remember to do so as soon as possible!
- It is important always to leave children with the assurance that adults are working hard to cure diseases. These are adult problems and children should be presented with a hopeful outlook for the future as you educate them.

36

~~~~~~

SEXUAL ABUSE AND PREVENTION

The topic of sexual abuse and its prevention must be addressed at home regardless of the discomfort parents feel about dealing with it. Informing children about the potential for sexual abuse, without causing unnecessary fears and anxieties, is one of the most difficult and delicate balances parents try to achieve. The health and safety of our children rest upon our success.

Children who have a healthy respect for their bodies are less likely to be victimized. This respect can be achieved by reinforcing your children's concept that their bodies are their own. Parents convey the notion of body privacy to their youngsters beginning as early as age three or four. By age five, the understanding of personal privacy should be well established.

Children should be reminded that the place to talk about private issues, such as sexual abuse, is at home with parents in a safe forum. It is not acceptable to share these private discussions with others. Review the differences between private and secret in Key 2 with your children, and remind them that their friends' parents will want to share private discussions with their kids, too, without outside intervention.

The subject of sexual abuse can be broached in the privacy of the home, most often during bath time. Your comments about how well your child's body is growing and your admiration of your youngster's good health can soften the topic of abuse. In the recent past, parents were encouraged to discriminate between "good" and "bad" touches as they defined abusive behavior. The current consensus is that labeling touches this way may be confusing to children in the long run. For instance, if it is a "bad touch" for someone to touch your daughter's breast, this notion may carry over into her adult life when the repercussions are undesirable. The following statements can be incorporated into a conversation with your child about the prevention of sexual abuse.

- "Gee, look how clean you are. What a healthy body you have!"
- "Now remember that your body is private, and no one should ask to touch or look at your body's private parts."
- "It's O.K. for us parents to help wash you or to look to see if you are hurt."
- "Your private body parts include your penis, your testicles, and your bottom. They are the parts covered by your bathing suit."
- "Your private body parts include your vagina, your clitoris, your bottom, and your breasts. They are all the parts covered by your bathing suit."

Children can feel good about their bodies if their parents are also respectful of boundaries. For instance, do not insist your children show affection just because you want them to, either by instructing that they kiss Aunt Janet, or by demanding hugs for yourself if they seem reluctant. To exercise such control in these instances sends mixed messages to children. On the one hand, you are asking your children not to allow others to touch their bodies, yet you are coercing them to show affection to others when you tell them to do so. Step back. They will learn to give and get affection when they feel it, according to what they have learned is appropriate.

There are times, though, when an adult, such as a physician, may need to look at or touch a child's private body parts for health reasons. If you anticipate a genital exam during a visit to your child's health care provider, you can prepare your child with the following explanation:

> "Louis, you know that no one should touch your private body parts in a way that makes you feel uncomfortable. Right? Today we will experience a different situation. One that's O.K. The physician/nurse needs to look at your genitals (or private body parts) to make sure you are healthy (or that everything is normal). I will be in the room with you, too."

You can alter this statement, leaving out or adding more details, as you see fit, depending upon your child's understanding, temperament, and your level of comfort.

NO/ GO/ TELL

If you have concerns about your child's sexual well-being, once you have reviewed the basic guidelines that define privacy, you can simply add: "Has anyone touched your private body parts in a way that has made you feel uncomfortable?"

If your child answers that such an incident has occurred, try to remain calm, and ask your youngster to tell you the whole story. Make sure you understand the content of it and are not misinterpreting in your anxiety. If you are not sure if the story is feasible, question more thoroughly, keeping your emotions under control. Do not blame your child or say anything that may be interpreted as a reproach. Your next step may be to seek professional help through your physician, local hospital, or local child protective services agency.

In the overwhelming majority of sexual molestation cases, the perpetrator is a person the child knows. Molesters can include people in the child's immediate or extended family, or baby-sitters, stepparents, neighbors, or others. Therefore, without frightening them, it is important that parents teach preventive measures to their children to ensure their safety from sexual abuse.

A relatively simple formula addresses prevention nicely. Your youngsters should know that if anyone touches them in ways that make them feel uncomfortable, they should say, "*No.*" Then they should "*Go.*" That means getting away from the perpetrator. Finally, they should "*Tell.*" Children should be encouraged to tell a parent or another trusted adult if they have been in a situation when molestation could have happened or did occur.

Even young children can comprehend this basic No/Go/ Tell concept. In addition, parents can arm their kids for action against abuse by playing the "what if" game. For example, you could ask, "What if a person at school asks you to show him your underwear or requests a hug or kiss. What would you do?" By readying children ahead of time, they will feel confident and inclined to practice No/Go/Tell should the occasion arise.

Assure your children it is never their fault if someone touches them inappropriately. Instead, it is the other person, acting unsuitably, who has broken the rules by invading a child's body and privacy. And be sure to allay youngsters' fears by pointing out that most adults are loving, caring people who would never think of hurting them.

Adults who sexually abuse children may tell their victims to keep the abuse a secret. It is seductive to a younger child to share a secret with an older perpetrator, particularly if the abusive adult has a prior relationship with the child. Parents should know their offspring's friends and must do everything possible to promote and encourage open communication. Secrets about sexual abuse can only be harmful. They enable the abuse to continue and they ensure the resulting scars will not be dealt with. (See the Suggested Readings for a list of easy-to-read picture books that parents can read with young children to help clarify the topic of secrets.)

As children get older, you may alert them to more specific behavior that provides them with clues to potential sexual molestation. Adapted from *When Sex Is the Subject* by Pamela Wilson, such clues include:

- Someone wants to look at or touch your body for no good reason.
- A bigger or stronger individual (child or adult) tries to get you to do something you don't want to do.
- You feel uncomfortable or have a funny feeling inside during a particular situation. Trust your instincts and do not go along. Tell a parent or trusted adult.
- A person tells you to keep a particular behavior a secret.
- You do something with another person, or that person does something to you. Afterward, you feel bad.

If parents suspect that their child has been sexually abused, they should seek help. Speak with your health care provider or your local hotline for support and for referrals to people who are specifically trained to deal with sexual abuse. Counseling and/or further evaluation may be necessary.

Children who have been sexually molested may or may not exhibit many overt signs of the abuse. As a rule, youngsters manifest underlying fear through behavioral changes. Although there is no single demeanor that demonstrates that your child may have been sexually victimized, the following are red flags:

- Compulsive, repetitive, sexual behavior, such as excessive masturbation, that preoccupies your child to the point he or she does not take part in other activities.
- A change in your child's normal disposition. Perhaps a normally playful youngster becomes consistently secretive or angry.
- A display of sexual behavior that is inappropriate for your child's age and our society's norms.
- An abrupt change in your child's normal social behavior, such as withdrawal and separation from family and/or friends.

Sexual abuse can have a lasting impact on your child's adult sexual health. As distressing as this criminal act is for parents of a victimized child, be assured it is ultimately far more distressing to your child. It is essential that parents: educate to prevent; encourage communication to elicit prompt reportage of significant events; watch for signs; emphasize your child's blamelessness; get help if your child is sexually abused.

37

GENDER ROLES

Sexuality is always about gender—the roles men and women adopt and the norms society teaches us about what is and is not permitted behavior in the playing out of these roles. Great care must be taken by vigilant parents to see that a child's gender and those preconceived societal roles based upon gender do not limit their offspring's future potential. For example, boys typically are encouraged to be assertive and ambitious, while girls are taught to be respectful and compliant. Such expectations can have detrimental repercussions in today's reality. For instance, we know assertiveness is required for success in the world. Girls, especially, challenged in their adulthood by the combined roles of motherhood and career, must learn to be assertive to compete with both males and other females as they strive to get jobs, build careers, and take care of their families. Another hurdle set up by traditional society is the narrow definition of some jobs and avocations as male, others as female.

Like most other aspects of child rearing, the effort to help youngsters experience their full capacities for growth and self-expression starts at home with parents. The following concepts can help parents address more equitable gender roles for young children:

• Both boys and girls should be valued equally as important human beings because they are.

- Girls and boys like to do some things that are the same and some things that are different. Each boy and each girl gets to choose what is fun and interesting.
- Not all girls are alike, just like not all boys are alike. Some girls play football; some boys play house.
- Both mothers and fathers can be loving caregivers.
- Men and women can do similar jobs.

Gender Roles at Home

Parents can inadvertently foster gender stereotypes subtly at home. For example, girls are "expected" to be sweet and nice; consequently, they are treated with more gentleness than their brothers. They may be encouraged to wear dresses, not pants. Boys, on the other hand, should not cry and are played with more roughly. Their clothes are purchased with an eye on durability. Mothers may be more eager to teach daughters to bake cookies while dads drag their young boys outside to throw a ball. The underlying messages here are clear even to young children, especially if they are not provided with opportunities to experience both types of behavior. It is still too rare that a parent tells a six-year-old boy, "Gee, you are so sweet!" or a four-year-old girl, "Gee, look how strong you are!"

Finally, though, there is good news. Male and female gender roles are beginning to blur in the home. This is cause for celebration! Fathers now take more active parts in parenting than in the past. Boys who see their fathers prepare meals, do laundry, and drive them to school will grow up assuming fewer gender-based labels on the duties of housekeeping and parenting. Girls who witness their mothers wielding a tool, checking the oil in the family car, or reading the *Wall Street Journal* will be similarly rewarded. In single-parent homes, it can be difficult finding opposite-sex role models for children, but resources such as churches, friends, neighbors, and community

organizations should be explored by single parents for potential role models.

Parents can best help their children develop healthy,
broad gender roles by modeling non-stereotypical roles for
them at home. Give your children equal opportunities to experience behavior and goals that in the past have been deemed
exclusively for the opposite gender. Both sexes can learn to
cook, fix their own bikes, nurture, and express the full range
of emotions.

Gender Roles and School

Although individual families may work hard to erase
male/female stereotypes at home, parents should be aware
that schools constantly bombard children with subtle, contradictory messages about gender roles.

Children spend most of their time in a school setting during their formative years, and the influence of this environment over youngsters cannot be ignored. Sexist messages still
exist in the classroom, and these should be identified and
addressed by parents, teachers, and curriculum developers.
In addition, teachers must be aware of the different ways in
which their teaching methods exclude or reinforce gender differences. For example are girls called on as frequently as boys
in class? Do teachers expect less from girls? Are boys given
more opportunities to have hands-on experiences than girls?
An excellent book that addresses this subject is *Failing at
Fairness* by Myra and David Sadker. The ways schools treat
girls and boys is an issue of debate and will continue to draw
attention as long as parents visit their children's classrooms
and stay involved in their youngsters formal education.

Gender Roles, the Media, and Toys

Commercial TV is loaded with sexism and gender stereotypes. Toys targeted toward girls are advertised routinely by

cute little girls with blond hair and make-up who play nicely indoors. Advertisements for boy's toys feature big action, loud noise, and highlight outdoor use. The children on TV playing with these toys are usually older and look more grown-up than the age group for which the toy is intended. Barbie teaches our daughters that she is the model of perfect feminine beauty. Her thinness and unrealistic body proportions are drawn and built—not real. If children watch kids on TV playing with gender-related toys in gender-related ways, they will come to believe they should emulate the TV propaganda in their own lives. A relatively new movement in TV programming portrays male children in caring and nurturing roles—occasionally. But TV advertisements that pay for the programs have not changed at all. The sexism that children are exposed to on commercial TV is blatant. (See Key 38 for more information on sexuality and TV.)

Keys to Help Parents Avoid Gender Traps

• Parents can point out professional role models working in their daughter's areas of interest. They can also demonstrate that male-dominated professions are also open to women.

• Show boys male role models who work in non-stereotypical professions such as nursing, or teaching. Point out that male artists, poets, and writers often work alone and express strong emotions through their art.

• Girls and boys should be encouraged to participate in household activities that have traditionally been labeled "boys'" or "girls'" work. Taking out the garbage, helping with meal preparation, doing the laundry, and so on, should not be restricted to a particular sex.

• Talk to girls about how to balance motherhood and career. If you are a working mother, show them how you handle both jobs, pointing out the difficulties and explaining how you have worked out those problems.

167

- Encourage girls to voice their opinions clearly, without apology.
- Boys should be encouraged to express the full range of their emotions and supported when they do so.
- Serve as a model, both as a woman and mother, for your children so they will expect to be treated well in future relationships. If you expect respect and commitment, and if you have a relationship with your spouse in which you negotiate and balance roles within the family, you will be your children's most powerful mentor.
- Serve as a model, both as a man and father, for your children. Show them how to treat future spouses, should they marry, and define how they should be treated by life partners. Participate fully in your youngsters' lives and encourage open communication. You will be their most powerful mentor.
- Let your daughter and son know how you feel about your own gender. Being proud of who you are as a person and as a parent provides your children with promising patterns for their own future identities.

As gender roles in our society are constantly redefined for future generations, both girls and boys need to be nurtured and validated in their pursuits, regardless of their gender. Gender categories must be flexible. Girls and boys should have the opportunity to share equally in resources and hopes for the future. As parents, we can be vigilant in order that youngsters are given the opportunities at school to maximize their potential. Growing up with parents who both are caretakers and nurturers with equal voices in the family is imperative for our kids' happy futures.

38

^^

SEXUALITY AND THE MEDIA

By now, parents are well aware that the media has an enormous impact on children's sexual development. It seems contradictory that in our society, where so many products of the media are steeped in sexual overtones, we try to teach children that sex is private. From a child's perspective, society does not appear to treat the subject of sexuality with any degree of privacy at all. From TV sitcoms, talk shows, soap operas, and commercials, to movies, video games, magazines, radio, music lyrics, and the internet, the media exploits sexuality with reckless abandon. These electronic communications often do not confirm parents' values and ethics; nevertheless, the media's role as an active sex educator of our children is a fact of life.

Of the media's various instruments, probably the TV is most pervasive in our children's lives. Nearly every home has one, and its screen illuminates our children's eyes, minds, and probably informs their choices on a daily basis. If we accept that TV *does* teach our kids, then the really important question for parents is, "What is it teaching?" The TV can be a remarkable, bright, entertaining friend, or it can be an excessively violent, sexually explicit foe that distorts real life and apparently champions shaky values.

On the average, kids watch approximately twenty-one hours of TV a week. Countless studies in pediatric literature have linked violence on TV with violent behavior among children. The rate of violent crime depicted on TV is about ten times greater than occurs in real life. It is not difficult to comprehend how violence on TV may promote aggressive behavior in children and desensitize them to acts of violence.

Medical literature also supports the connection between poor school performance and childhood obesity in those children who spend inordinate amounts of time watching TV.

Television and Sexuality

Many popular sitcoms on commercial TV are full of sexual overtures, even when the situation portrays what would normally be a nonsexual relationship between the characters. The background audience's mocking laughter, combined with the characters' humorous sexual innuendoes, suggest there is something taboo in every interaction.

A clear dichotomy exists between parents and TV networks. On the one hand, parents attempt to set sexual guidelines through their own behavior, showing strong commitment to one another and a joint sense of responsibility to themselves, each other, and to their children. On the other hand, the television teaches youngsters that sexuality is something to be made fun of and taken lightly. In addition, it overemphasizes the centrality of sex in daily adult living. Too often, the clear message on TV is that all we adults think about is sex and violence. Little mention, if any, is made about responsible decisions or future consequences when sexual encounters occur among TV characters.

Television and Reality

There are other reasons to maintain a watchful eye on the types of media material that bombard children. Youngsters' perceptions of characters on TV are unrealistic because the television's version of humanity lacks much resemblance to real people living real lives. Males are overrepresented; whites outnumber minorities; and professionals, such as lawyers, doctors, and athletes, are often glamorized. Characters wear designer clothes and make-up; blemishes and wrinkles are erased by trick lighting. Fake beauty oozes across our screens. Unrealistic financial pictures of ordinary people are represented as the norms of society. Fantasies about glamorous lives supplant reality, and the simple tales about people's struggles to reach the common goals of everyday life are rarely portrayed. Children are mesmerized by these fairy tale representations of real life, and they are influenced by them. This type of TV programming affects the ways youngsters view themselves and the world around them.

In addition, the media romanticizes relationships to a point where the lines between love, sexual attraction, infatuation, and friendships are grossly blurred. Problems are solved in a matter of minutes, with little discussion about the consequences of irresponsible choice and action, and no character is left feeling hurt or misunderstood for long. Every aspect of life has an easy, clear-cut solution and, of course, there is always a happy ending. Explanations are seldom offered about how decisions are made and conclusions reached.

The morals and beliefs that stream through the TV set and infiltrate our children's minds are not always ethical. Situations that adults, who can separate truth from fiction, can recognize as fantasies, confuse a young ten-year-old and plant seeds of powerful belief systems that can damage future relationships.

Key Points about Family TV Viewing
- Avoid using television as a baby-sitter or as a dinner companion. Children who spend time in front of the TV watching unmonitored material are likely to lose track of what is appropriate behavior in human interactions.

- Although movie videos are an alternative to television, make sure the rating and content are appropriate for your child's age. Many videos, even Disney's, are typically male-dominated with females and males often playing gender stereotyped roles.
- Do spend time with your child watching educational programs. Public broadcasting channels are excellent and provide many child-oriented programs.
- Set a good example for your children through your own TV habits. Parents who come home and sit in front of the TV are sending a loud message about the relative unimportance of family life. Your example is always your child's primary model.
- Monitor your child's TV viewing. Be critical and selective. Learn to evaluate the programming and advertising your children are exposed to. Be media literate.
- Turn the TV off when not watching it, as opposed to leaving it on all the time.
- Point out to your child how toy advertisements make playthings appear better than they really are. If possible, purchase an item and compare the ad's claims with its true characteristics.
- Talk back to the TV. Be an active viewer. If your children see that you are critical of the screen content, they might learn to do the same.
- View programs with your child and use the situations presented in them as opportunities to review values and sensitive topics, such as sex, AIDS, and unethical behavior.
- Provide the older child with the opportunity to decide how much time to watch TV. According to the American Academy of Pediatrics, an average of one to two quality hours per day is reasonable. This might be meted out in hour-long increments throughout the week or accumulated for use

over the weekend. As children get older, they must become their own monitor.

- If you view an inappropriate program, or one that does not support your family's values, let the network know. If enough parents send in comments, programming will change.
- Write to the networks to voice your concerns. (See Additional Resources for addresses of TV networks and organizations that help promote better TV for children.)

Not all TV is bad. Valuable documentaries and family programming often address sensitive issues such as teen pregnancy, AIDS, divorce, and human relationships, and some TV is valuable simply because it is entertaining. But like any outside influence in our children's lives, television can become too pervasive. Quantity and quality seem the keys to its successful presence in children's lives.

39

PARENTING:
CHALLENGING
RESPONSIBILITY

P arenting is by far the most demanding job most adults will ever undertake. Yet, in our society, children are having children long before they are capable of raising them. Our kids, of course, must understand that sex, especially unprotected sex, leads to babies. Babies, in turn, lead to long careers of parenting. Perhaps we parents could prevent more child pregnancies if we worked harder to teach our youngsters how much different and more difficult it is to raise a baby than it is to nurture a doll. Perhaps sexuality training could include more material about the demands of parenthood.

The task of parenting should be seen as a challenging climb by parents guiding their children to a distant, high peak. The trip itself is satisfying and enjoyable, but requires constant diligence to avoid the gaping crevices and loose footholds along the way. Each step involves parents' best decision-making skills. We enjoy the company of other parents, children, teachers, and friends along the way who can alter our journeys significantly—helping or hindering as we allow. But final responsibility is up to us parents to achieve the goal, the peak, for our youngsters. We hope to help them become the best they can be for themselves and for their society. This is a challenging task for two, caring adults, more difficult for a single parent, and nearly impossible for teen moms and dads.

If the career of parenting sounds a bit lonely, it is. In the past, raising a family was accomplished with the help of extended family members who lived upstairs, next door, or around the corner. But, as a result of societal changes, family members have separated and are spread over great distances. Therefore, loving resources that were available for teaching children, disciplining, potty training, and talking about the "birds and the bees" have been dispersed. Parents today must learn how to parent on their own. Our society has scrambled to make up the deficit by authoring books about childrearing, establishing classes and phone hot lines, and inundating us with talk shows that demonstrate scary instances of parent/child relationships gone wrong. The hard truth is that, unlike all other careers, there is no agreed-upon course of training for becoming a successful parent. We must choose among the diverse mini-courses, hoping for success with no degree. If this is a mind-boggling circumstance for mature adults, it is impossible for children playing at being parents.

As parents raise their families, they feel an enormous sense of accountability and, hopefully, great joy inherent in the job. There are, of course, huge demands on time and physical energy. In addition, meeting the minimum financial requirements to feed, clothe, shelter, and educate a youngster is an awesome task and requires pre-planning and an appropriate education in order to find a job to meet the needs of a family. Generally, only a few days pass before new parents feel the dizzying tilting between worrisome responsibility for their kids' well-being and the overwhelming glee at their very presence. But when teenagers put themselves in the role of parents, the teeter-totter only tilts in one direction, weighed down by the boulder of responsibility. Clearly, raising babies should

175

be the happy labor of mature parents who can and will commit to lifetime relationships with their kids that provide pleasure and joy for all of them. It is our duty to convey this message to our children.

Parenting and the Preschooler

The foundation of children's self-esteem and their sense of self-worth is established during these early years. The ways in which they are cared for, listened to, played with, and taught are crucial to children's healthy, sexual development.

During this stage, children feel a strong sense that they are the centers of their parent's world, and they demand a great deal of parents' energy.

Although preschoolers cannot understand the complexities of parenting, most of them assume they will grow up to be mommies and daddies themselves someday. They watch their parent's relating as husband and wives and as caretakers of their children, and they emulate these roles during their play with other youngsters. They dramatize that they *do* assimilate behavior exhibited around them.

In the meantime parents watch, set rules, monitor, and grapple with the sexual values they want to convey as their children grow out of childhood's fantasy and toward the reality of possible parenthood. They are certainly affected by their parents' involvement during these early years.

Parenting and the Preteen

As children enter their preteen years, parenting styles that once worked may no longer be effective. Just as you relax, thinking you have the rules set and have figured out the game, changes occur. Needs are different. Preteen youngsters become more independent but, at the same time, still require supervision. At this age, there is a brief period when you can show your kids dramatically what is entailed in bringing up a family. So make teachable moments of this opportunity.

Children should participate in family chores from early age. Work gives the child a sense of oneness with the family unit as well as a feeling of personal accomplishment. The value of family life is more concretely spelled out the more actively a child participates. Therefore, the older the child, the more involved he or she should be in the everyday goals and concerns of the family as a whole. As children share more fully in everyday family responsibilities, parents can point out how difficult it is to take on the task of parenting as well as handling the day-to-day running of a busy household.

Youngsters can understand, with a little guidance, how being a parent is a lifelong commitment with wonderful rewards but also never-ending accountability. For instance, children with some responsibility for baby-sitting soon learn that they cannot do a good job and accomplish other things at the same time, such as talking on the phone or watching TV. In addition, preteens are old enough to know that families make choices based upon financial considerations. Camping vacations, less expensive than other options, may be elected for that reason. Casseroles may be more abundant on family dinner tables than chops. Point out why this is the case. As kids get older, clothing budgets might be a good way to show that money is not an elastic commodity. Children can hear that college education is a huge expenditure that must be planned for from the birth of a child. Therefore, for many reasons, we parents opt to save rather than spend. Sometimes we even have to work more than one job to make ends meet.

Having a family is a difficult task that takes plenty of hard work, money, and a degree of emotional stability that only comes with time. Point out to your child that becoming a teenage parent is not a good choice. Once a teenager has a child, life changes drastically. Schooling is interrupted, job opportunities are limited; there are no summer breaks from parenting, and a typical teenage social life is no longer feasible. Show and tell your preteens as many reasons as you can think of that will help them actively choose against early pregnancy. Parenting a baby is not an easy task, even for an adult who is stable and married. For a teen, pregnancy and parenting have enormous consequences.

Key Points about Parenting

- Parenting is a very demanding responsibility that requires two committed adults whenever possible.
- Parenting a child is a lifelong experience that can be very fulfilling.
- There are many different parenting styles. No one style is right or wrong.
- Taking a hard look at our personal parenting styles, and those of our parents, can help us be better parents for our own children.
- Parents need support from other family and community members.
- Teenagers are not ready for the financial or emotional responsibilities that come with parenting.

QUESTIONS AND ANSWERS

How do I explain the meaning of alternative expressions for intercourse when my children use words like *fuck*?

It's always good to find out first where your child learned the term, and asking may buy you some time to catch your breath. One possible response could be: "*Fuck* is another word for sexual intercourse, but it is used in a derogatory sense or to hurt someone's feelings. It is unkind or, at the least, crude. This word also is used to refer to intercourse between animals. It places the act of sexual intercourse on an animal level—one that is not associated with love. It is therefore belittling when it is associated with the human act of sexual intercourse."

A close family member is having a baby and is not married. How should I explain this to my children if they ask?

Similar situations to the one you describe will arise on TV, so being prepared to explain pregnancy out of marriage is important. You may say something like: "If a man and a woman have intercourse, the woman can get pregnant. Becoming a parent is a very big responsibility. It's better if two committed parents bring up a child. A single parent may find raising a baby to be very difficult."

You may want to state your own values at this point. Some may include:

- "I believe that it is important to be married before having a baby."
- "We feel that sexual intercourse is only for adults, not teenagers."
- "We hope that you will wait until you are married before having sex and starting a family."

What should I do if I find pornographic magazines in my son's or daughter's room?

First of all, how were these magazines obtained? Were they purchased by the youngster, discovered at home, or given to him by a friend? Your main approach should be guided by your personal values. If these magazines are part of your household reading matter, you may have to do some explaining. Pornography most often exploits females for the exclusive benefit of sexual pleasure. Pornographic magazines display raw nudity and sexuality devoid of messages about commitment, responsibility, or relationships. Often, unlike nudity in paintings reproduced in art books, an element of sleaziness is present. Understand that your child most likely is driven by his curiosity of the forbidden and unknown and by his sex drive! If you don't raise the roof when you find the magazines, you'll be much better off. Ask your son or daughter to ask any questions about those magazine photographs, and use the opportunity to convey your values about pornography and sexuality. Provide him with alternative books and magazines that you think are more suitable, but expect that he may well return to explicit materials for titillation. And that's pretty normal.

How should I answer when my child asks, "Why *do* people have sex anyway?"

Many children, especially at the prepubertal stage, have a hard time understanding why adults have sexual intercourse. Parents can explain to their children that babies are produced when people have intercourse, and without more new babies, the human race would die out. Parents may want to include their own beliefs about the sanctity of life. In addition, preteens can begin to understand that everyone is born with the capacity to enjoy sexual feelings. These feelings are exciting, new, and at times can become very powerful and pleasurable. Engaging in sexual intercourse is a way that adults share loving feelings toward each other. Nevertheless, big feelings that involve big actions (sexual intercourse) have big consequences. These are concepts that merit frequent review.

How are twins conceived?

Usually when a woman ovulates only one egg cell is released. But occasionally, two egg cells (or three, four, etc.) are released and each may be fertilized by a sperm. Each fertilized egg cell develops into a baby. These are known as fraternal twins. They can be girls, boys, or a girl and a boy. They will look like siblings. Certain medications and heredity can enhance a woman's chances of having a multiple birth.

On the other hand, one egg cell may be released and fertilized. During the division process it may divide into two equal parts from which two identical babies grow. These are identical twins. There is nothing a woman can consciously do to have identical twins.

What *is* the proper age to have sex?

Many preteens are still very concrete in their thinking and feel that there is a right age or a right time for sex to take place. If we parents just tell them the answer we believe is the correct one, they will abide by it—maybe. But we adults know that reality is fraught with roadblocks to our good intentions. Peer pressure, the media, and issues of self-esteem can override parents' best answers. In fact, sexual intercourse is not an age-dependent activity. In matters of sex, other issues such as personal responsibility, commitment to a partner, and for many, marriage, determine what activity is appropriate.

How and at what age should I explain orgasms to my youngsters?

An orgasm can be difficult to explain. When boys enter puberty they will begin to experience orgasms if and when they have wet dreams. Girls can also have orgasms although there is not an ejaculation associated with them. When parents start to talk to their youngsters about puberty and the physical changes that accompany it, there is no way to avoid the topic of orgasms.

Explain to your children that orgasms are a series rhythmic contractions that are felt mostly in the genital area and are very pleasurable. These feelings are felt as throbbing sensations that spread through the whole body, causing intense pleasure. After orgasms, people feel very relaxed.

A youngster once said to me: "I guess an orgasm is like the punch line of the joke!"

How can I help my youngster feel comfortable talking to me about sex?

Encourage your child to talk to you about anything, and really mean that. Keep an open mind, and watch your body language. Subtle gestures that project your own discomfort will send your child scurrying for safety. Humor is helpful— but ridicule is very damaging. Children hate lectures. You can be most effective as a good listener, not a preacher. You can answer questions put to you without confusing your child with extraneous information. At the end of the conversation, hug and assure your youngster you are glad he or she chose to come to you.

While taking a shower, my young child asks if he can touch my genitals. How should I handle this situation?

Children are naturally curious about adults' bodies, especially that of the opposite sex. If your child asks to touch your genitals, breasts, and so on, you should calmly explain that your body is private and therefore you do not want them to touch it; that is why people wear clothes. An incident like this may guide you away from showering with your youngster. This may be the appropriate time to set some boundaries surrounding privacy and modesty at home.

GLOSSARY

Anus (AY-nuss)   the posterior opening of the intestinal tract where the bowel movements come out.

Bladder (BLAD-er)   a sac-like structure in the lower abdomen that holds urine.

Buttocks (BUT-toks)   the two large muscles that cover the anus.

Cervix (SER-viks)   the narrow lower or outer end of the uterus. This opening connects the uterus to the vagina.

Circumcision (sir-come-SISH-un)   the cutting off of the prepuce of males.

Clitoris (CLIT-uh-riss)   a small erectile organ at the anterior part of the vulva.

Cricoid (CRICK-oid)   a cartilage of the larynx, also known as "Adam's apple."

Ejaculation (ee-jack-you-LAY-shun)   the sudden or spontaneous discharging of semen from the penis.

Erection (ee-RECK-shun)   occurs when a previous flaccid penis becomes firm and erect.

Estrogen (ES-troh-jen)   a hormone produced by the ovaries. It is responsible for the outward signs of puberty in girls.

Genitals (JEN-i-tulls)   a person's sexual organs.

Glans (GLANZ)   the crown or distal portion of the penis.

Gynecomastia (gi-na-coe-MAS-tia)   excessive development of the breast in the male.

Hormones (HOR-moans)   a substance that circulates in body fluids and produces specific effects on different parts of the body.

Hymen (HI-men)   a thin tissue that partly or wholly closes the opening of the vagina.

Labia (LAY-bee-a)   fatty folds that cover the vulva.

Menarche (meh-NAR-key)   a girl's first menstrual period.

Mons (MONZ)   the portion of fatty tissue that covers the pubic bone.

Orgasm (OR-gaz-um)   the climax of sexual excitement that is usually accompanied in the male by ejaculation.

Ova (OH-vah)   the plural form of ovum.

Ovum (OH-vum)   a female's egg cell.

Penis (PEE-niss)   the male's sexual organ that hangs between his legs.

Perineum (peh-re-KNEE-um)   the area between the scrotum and the anus in males, and between the posterior vulva and anus in females.

Prepuce (PREE-pyoos)   the loose fold of skin that covers the glans of the penis.

Prostate gland (PRAHS-tate)   a male gland located at the base of the bladder. It contributes a thin, milky fluid that makes up part of the semen.

Puberty (PEW-bur-tee)   the period of becoming first capable of reproducing sexually, marked by maturing of the genitals and secondary sex characteristics.

Pubic (PEW-bik) the anterior part of the hip bones.

Rectum (REK-tum) the last part of the intestine, which connects to the anus.

Scrotum (SKROH-tum) the external pouch or sac that holds the testicles.

Sebum (SEE-bom) an oily lubricant substance made by glands under the skin.

Semen (SEA-men) a thick, whitish fluid of the male's reproductive organ that contains sperm.

Testicles (TES-ti-kuls) the two round or almond-shaped structures that hang below the penis and are responsible for making sperm.

Testosterone (tess-TOSS-ter-own) a male hormone that is produced by the testicles.

Urethra (yuh-REE-thra) a tubelike canal that carries off the urine from the body and in the male serves also to carry semen from the penis.

Vagina (vah-JIE-nah) a canal that connects the uterus to the woman's outer sex organs. The vagina is also known as the birth canal.

Vas deferens (Vas-DEF-a-renz) the two tubes that allow sperm to pass from the testicles.

Vulva (VUL-va) the external parts of the female's genital organs.

SUGGESTED READINGS

For Young Preschoolers

Cole, Joanna. *How You Were Born.* New York: William Morrow, 1984.

Gordon, Sol. *Girls Are Girls and Boys Are Boys, So What's the Difference?* Amherst, NY: Prometheus Books, 1991.

Gordon, Sol, and Judith Gordon. *Did the Sun Shine Before You Were Born? A Sex Education Primer.* Amherst, NY: Prometheus Books, 1992.

Jennings, Donna A. *Baby Brendon's Busy Day: A Sexuality Primer.* Tallahassee, FL: Goose Pond Publishing, 1993.

———. *Baby Brenda's Busy Day: A Sexuality Primer.* Tallahassee, FL: Goose Pond Publishing, 1993.

Kransny Brown, Laurie, Ed.D., and Marc Brown. *What's the Big Secret, Dinosaurs? A Guide to Sex for Girls and Boys.* New York: Little, Brown and Company, 1997.

Mayle, Peter. *Where Did I Come From?* Secaucus, NJ: Carol Publishing Group, 1973.

Schoen, Mark. *Bellybuttons Are Navels.* Amherst, NY: Prometheus Books, 1990.

For Preteens

Jukes, Mavis. *It's A Girl Thing—How To Stay Healthy, Safe and in Charge*. New York: Alfred A. Knopf, 1996.

Bourgeois, Paulette, and Martin Wolfish, M.D. *Changes in You and Me: A Book About Puberty, Mostly for Boys*. Toronto, Ontario: Somerville House, 1994.

Harris, Robie H. *It's Perfectly Normal: Changing Bodies, Growing Up, Sex and Sexual Health*. Cambridge, MA: Candlewick Press, 1994.

Madaras, Lynda. *The What's Happening to My Body Book for Girls*. New York: Newmark Press, 1988.

———. *The What's Happening to My Body Book for Boys*. New York: Newmark Press, 1988.

Gardner-Loulan, JoAnn, Bonnie Lopez, and Marcia Quackenbush. *Period*. Volcano, CA: Volcano Press, 1990.

Thomson, Ruth. *Have You Started Yet?* Los Angeles: Price Stern Sloan, 1995.

Bell, Alison, and Lisa Rooney, M.D. *Your Body, Yourself: A Guide to Your Changing Body*. Chicago: Contemporary Books, 1996.

Virtue, Doreen. *Your Emotions, Yourself: A Guide to Your Changing Emotions*. Chicago: Contemporary Books, 1996.

Mayle, Peter. *What's Happening to Me?* Secaucus, NJ: Carol Publishing Group, 1975.

For Parents of Young Children

American Social Health Association. *Becoming an Askable Parent—How To Talk with Your Child about Sexuality*. 1994.

Bernstein, Anne C. *Flight of the Stork: What Children Think (and When) About Sex and Family Building.* Indianapolis, IN: Perspectives Press, 1994.

Calderone, Mary S., and Johnson, Eric W. *The Family Book about Sexuality.* New York: Harper Collins, 1990.

Goldman, Ronald, and Goldman, Juliette. *Show Me Yours: Understanding Children's Sexuality.* Australia: Penguin, 1988.

Planned Parenthood Federation of America. *How To Talk with Your Child about Sexuality: A Parent's Guide.* 1993.

———. *Human Sexuality: What Children Should Know and When They Should Know It.* 1996.

———. *Talking About Sex: A Guide For Families.* 1996.

Wilson, Pamela M. *When Sex Is The Subject: Attitudes and Answers for Young Children.* Santa Cruz, CA: ETR Associates, 1991.

HIV/AIDS (For Parents of Young Children)

American Academy of Pediatrics. *Know the Facts About HIV and AIDS: Guidelines for Parents.* 1995.

Quackenbush, Marcia, and Sylvia Villareal, M.D. *Does AIDS Hurt? Educating Young Children About AIDS.* Santa Cruz, CA: Network Publications, 1992.

Sexuality Information and Education Council of the US (SIECUS). *How to Talk to Your Children About AIDS.* 1994.

Sexual Abuse Prevention

Gordon, Sol, and Judith Gordon. *A Better Safe Than Sorry Book: A Family Guide for Sexual Assault Prevention.* Prometheus Books, 1990.

KCRR Staff, and Jennifer Fay. *"He Told Me Not to Tell." A Parent's Guide for Talking to Your Child about Sexual Assault.* KCSA Research Center, 1979.

Abstinence

Howard, Marion. *How To Help Your Teenager Postpone Sexual Involvement.* New York: The Continuum Publishing Company, 1988.

Napier, Kristine. *The Power of Abstinence. How Parents Can Help Teens Postpone Sexual Activity—& Achieve Emotional Security, Maximum Self-Esteem, & Stay Healthy.* New York: Avon Books, 1996.

Abstinence, ABC. Pamphlet by ETR Associates.*

Gender (For Parents)

Sadker, Myra, and David Sadker. *Failing at Fairness: How America's Schools Cheat Girls.* New York: Charles Scribner's Sons, 1994.

Paley, V. G. *Boys & Girls: Superheroes in the Doll Corner.* Chicago: University of Chicago Press, 1984.

Rites of Passage

Imbed-Black, Evan, Ph.D., and Canine Robbers, Ed.D. *Rituals for Our Times: Celebrating, Healing, and Changing Our Lives and Our Relationships.* New York: Harper Collins Publishers, 1992.

---

*ETR Associates provides many other pamphlets for parents and young children. Call 1-800-321-4407 for information, or write to P.O. Box 1830, Santa Cruz, CA 95061-1830.

Roessel, Monty. *Kinaaldá: A Navajo Girl Grows Up.* Minneapolis, MN: Lerner Publications Company, 1993.

TV and the Media

Strasburge, Victor, M.D. *Adolescents and the Media.* Thousand Oaks, CA: Sage Publications, 1995.

Wallace, Shelagh. *The TV Book: The Kids' Guide To Talking Back.* Buffalo, NY: Annick Press, 1996.

Parenting

Eyre, Linda, and Richard Eyre. *Teaching Your Children Values.* New York: Fireside, 1993.

Cline, Foster, M.D., and Jim Fay. *Parenting with Love and Logic: Teaching Children Responsibility.* Colorado Springs, CO: Pinon Press, 1990.

Gordon, Thomas. *P.E.T.: Parent Effectiveness Training.* New York: New American Library, 1975.

ADDITIONAL RESOURCES

Videos

What Kids Want To Know About Sex and Growing Up. Produced by Children's Television Network. A wonderful video to view with children dealing with the changes of puberty. Created for families with children eight to twelve years of age.

How To Talk with Your Young Child About Sex . . . and Why It's Important. Produced by Strengthening Family Ties, 1992. This video addresses sensitive issues related to sex and young children. An excellent resource for families who are unsure about how to start talking to young children about sexuality. Write to SFT, P.O. Box 192, Holt, MI 48842.

Talking About Sex—A Guide for Families. An excellent video produced by Planned Parenthood Federation of America, Inc., It also includes a Parent's Guide and Activity Book for families of pre-teens and teens.

Information Hotlines

National AIDS Hotline
(800) 342-AIDS or (342-2437)
(800) 344-7432 (Spanish)

National Child Abuse Hotline
(800) 422-4453

Growing Up Healthy Hotline
(800) 522-5006

Planned Parenthood Federation of America, Inc.
(800) 230-PLAN
(Automatically connects callers to Planned Parenthood health center nearest them)

National Child Abuse Hotline
(800) 422-4453

Parents Anonymous Hotline
(800) 421-0353

Organizations

Sexuality Information and
Education Council of the US
(SIECUS)
130 West 42nd Street,
Suite 2500
New York, NY 10036
(212) 819-9770
SIECUS provides numerous services to help communities de-
sign and implement sexuality
and HIV/AIDS programs. There
are library services, member-
ship, and publications available.

Parents, Families, and Friends
of Lesbians and Gays (PFLAG)
1101 14th Street NW #1030
Washington, DC 20005
(202) 638-4200

Planned Parenthood
Federation of America, Inc.
810 Seventh Avenue
New York, NY 10019
(212) 541-7800

National AIDS Clearinghouse
P.O. Box 6003
Rockville, MD 20849
(800) 458-5231

Girls Inc.
30 East 33rd Street
New York, NY 10016-5394
(212) 689-3700

National PTA
2000 L Street NW, Suite 600
Washington, DC 20036
(202) 331-1380

Organizations Related to the Media

Center For Media Literacy
4727 Wilshire Blvd., #403
Los Angeles, CA 90010
(800) 226-9494
FAX 213-931-4474
Web site: http:/www.earthlink.-
net/cml
This organization is dedicated
to helping children and adults
become aware of the media's influence in our daily lives. It
teaches specific skills for critical viewing of all aspects of the
media. An excellent resource
for any information related to
the media.

Cable in the Classroom
1900 N Beauregard Street,
Suite 108
Alexandria, VA 22311
(800) 743-5355
This organization offers critical
viewing workshops, called Taking Charge of Your TV, which
teaches parents, children, and
educators to view TV with a
critical eye.

Center for Media Education
and Campaign for Kids' TV
1511 K Street, NW, Suite 518
Washington, DC 20005
The Campaign for Kids' TV is
committed to improving the
quality of children's television,
educating the public about the
effects of TV, and empowering

parents and educators to deal more effectively with the media.

TV Parental Guidelines
P.O. Box 14097
Washington, DC 20004
(202) 879-9364

Magazine for Preteens Girls

New Moon: The Magazine for Girls and Their Dreams
P.O. Box 3620
Duluth, MN 55803-3620
(800) 381-4743
e-mail:
newmoon@newmoon.duluth.mn
This is an international magazine for every girl who wants her voice heard and her dreams taken seriously. *New Moon* celebrates girls, explores the passage from girl to woman, and builds healthy resistance to gender inequities.

INDEX